A Very Human Jesus

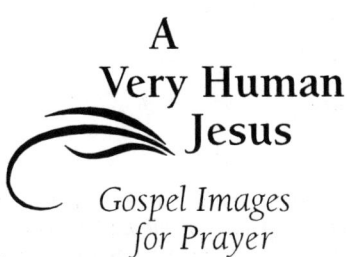

Gospel Images for Prayer

MARK

by Robert L. Knopp

Foreword by Robert F. Morneau

PAULINE
BOOKS & MEDIA

Nihil Obstat:
Rev. Thomas W. Buckley, STD, SSL

Imperatur:
†Bernard Cardinal Law
Archbishop of Boston
June 10, 1996

The Scripture quotations contained herein are from the *New Revised Standard Version Bible: Catholic Edition,* copyright © 1996 and 1989 by the Division of Christian Education of the National Council of Churches of Christ in the U.S.A. Used by permission. All rights reserved.

Cover design: Sergia Ballini, FSP

ISBN 0-8198-3085-2

Copyright © 1998, Daughters of St. Paul

Printed and published in the U.S.A. by Pauline Books & Media, 50 Saint Pauls Avenue, Boston MA 02130-3491.

http://www.pauline.org

Pauline Books & Media is the publishing house of the Daughters of St. Paul, an international congregation of women religious serving the Church with the communications media.

1 2 3 4 5 6   03 02 01 00 99 98

Contents

Foreword
9

Invitation
13

The Public Ministry of Jesus

21

The Passion and Resurrection

161

Foreword

A fierce battle is taking place in our culture regarding the imagination. Nor is this a *cold* war but one of extreme passion and intensity. The importance of victory cannot be exaggerated because the images we create or absorb shape our inner attitudes, which in turn radically influence our lifestyle and behavior. It's a simple syllogism but one which has profound ramifications.

Images come from multiple sources: television, songs, movies, magazines, science, poetry, lived lives. Within the Christian community a major source stimulating the imagination is sacred Scripture. God's word often draws pictures for us that contain values and virtues that lead us to the kingdom: Jesus as good shepherd; our spirituality as one of mutual self-giving as depicted in the vine and the branches; the separation of the sheep and the goats based on our treatment of one another; God as the potter shaping and molding our lives.

In a world filled with incredible violence, the Christian community continues to offer an alternative to the culture of death. Ours is to be a culture of love, a "civilization of love," in which every single human being is invited to the wedding feast and must be treated with awesome respect. The poet Gerard Manley Hopkins calls us "immortal diamonds." Our images must offer realistic hope.

It is not enough to encounter an image, symbol, metaphor or story. More is required. We must assimilate and appropriate these formative sights and sounds until they are absorbed into our spiritual bloodstream. This will require prayer and reflection as well as commitment to translate them into action. Our process of formation and conversion takes time and much grace. Perseverance in prayer is essential to Christian maturity.

This volume, like its three companions, is about discipleship and how we respond to that call by using biblical images. Robert Knopp looks deeply into each of the Gospels and extracts for us images that give us access to the person of Jesus. Each Gospel is unique in its approach to the Lord but all are the same in inviting us to know, love and serve him with all of our being.

In *A Very Human Jesus*, we prayerfully ponder our Lord close up. We can feel his anger and surprise, identify with his grief and joy. Just like us, he suffers and is tired; he has to deal with frustration and disappointment. Yet in all his rich humanity we are given access to Jesus who is truly divine.

The gift of faith empowers us to come to know Jesus the Christ as he truly is.

One last word about images, the cornerstone of this book. Thomas Merton once stated that the imagination is one means for "keeping the object of our belief before our minds." One of our contemporary illnesses is forgetfulness. If we forget who Jesus is and what he does for us, we are truly in danger of getting lost in the cosmos. Images help us to remember and more, how to live as disciples of the Lord.

†ROBERT F. MORNEAU
Auxiliary Bishop of Green Bay

Invitation

Let's look together into the Gospel of Mark, focusing on his images to ponder and pray. For Mark's images can awaken our minds to think and move our hearts to pray as Jesus did.

If we accept the judgment of most modern scholars that Mark wrote the earliest Gospel, we may suppose his images to be the closest to those by which the apostles presented Jesus and perhaps even to those Jesus himself used in his teaching. That assumption seems reinforced by Mark's more vivid portrayal of Jesus' actions and especially reactions—his emotions, frustrations, fatigue, suffering. In contrast, Matthew stands off at a greater distance, reverencing the Messiah's words and acts. Luke concentrates upon Jesus' compassion for those in need and his joyful embrace of life, while John conducts us more deeply into the mystery of Jesus' divinity.

For simple contemplation of Jesus, I like Mark. Although Matthew and Luke repeat most of the content of Mark's Gospel, they depict less graphically than he the Jesus who is so fully human that he shares our feelings and limitations, even as he mysteriously manifests his divinity. Those human emotions and limitations—not character flaws—are of great importance to us, for we tend to lose sight of Jesus' humanity, or even to drown it in his divinity.

Thus, Mark's Jesus is the Christ most accessible to us. And Mark assures us that in finding his very human Jesus, we find God himself. When the high priest asks whether he is the Son of God, Mark's Jesus responds, "I am, and 'you will see the Son of Man seated at the right hand of the Power [God]'" (Mk 14:62, referring to Dan 7:13-14). Even the centurion, who watched Jesus die, exclaims: "Truly this man was God's Son!" (Mk 15:39).

In the Old Testament, the prophets who spoke God's word to his people yearned to see his face. In Mark's Gospel, we see God's face in Jesus at closest range—a face expressing joy and grief, surprise and anger. Thus, Mark encourages us to speak freely to his Jesus until he becomes *our* Jesus. He does this with an admirable simplicity, often by expressing or suggesting images that appeal to our own human experience. But Mark is also subtle, raising questions without offering easy answers. With a few deft touches he leads us into amazing depths, then leaves us to muse, marvel—and pray.

Unfortunately, we may easily miss many of Mark's subtle implications, perhaps because we are unfamiliar with the Old Testament passages he uses as background or because we are so familiar with his general gospel message that we pass too rapidly over the images through which he presents the good news. To find his very human Jesus, I have tried to develop in these pages the images he presents or merely suggests, and to explore some of the meanings they convey or imply.

Imagery usually appeals to our senses through rich color, form and sound, but the evangelists offer us no descriptive details of Jesus' external appearance and few such images of his actions. They prefer the symbolic imagery of narratives and parables that suggest the spiritual sense or inner mystery of Jesus' life, words and actions. Through such images rather than abstract statements, Mark invites us to enter prayerfully into Jesus' mystery. I have therefore divided his Gospel into units in which I find a central image or cluster of images that can stir our musing.

In my own musings upon these images and their implications, I have tried to be true to Mark and his Jesus. Although Mark's writing is not poetic in its use of the external devices we usually associate with poetry, it is the essence of poetry in its use of images to suggest feelings and meanings far beneath its verbal surface. To convey something of the "feel" of Mark and to respond to his implied invitation to pray, I have therefore used free-flowing, often rhythmic sense lines intended to harmonize with Mark's tone and to reflect his simple, sometimes redundant style in portraying Jesus' profound humanity and suffering.

Poetic expression can be such a powerful vehicle for conveying meaning and emotion that it risks distracting attention from the poem's content. I have therefore rarely used poetry's most self-conscious devices, such as rhyme and assonance, which are too often achieved only at the expense of obscuring meaning. I hope my efforts to turn an apt phrase, balance lines or strike an appropriate rhythm emphasize Mark's meaning, yet never detract from it.

Without trying to explain difficult passages, I have at times used the interpretations of Matthew and Luke, who seem not only to have used Mark's content but often to have clarified or modified his meaning by recasting his more difficult passages and broadening his perhaps too narrow portrayal of Jesus' personality. I have occasionally had recourse also to John and other New Testament authors as Mark's authentic interpreters, for the Church gathered their works with Mark's to constitute, along with the Old Testament, its sacred books. Like a rich garden, these Scriptures feature many beautiful beds of varicolored plants and flowers, all cultivated by the Holy Spirit to fit together in revealing Jesus with the Father and the Spirit—and ourselves as God's people. Mark's

Gospel truly blossoms when seen against the backdrop of the entire scriptural canon, which offers background and highlighting to illuminate his most colorful passages.

In the relatively few passages over which Christian churches still differ, I have adhered to the Catholic Church's interpretation of the apostolic traditions that gave rise to the New Testament. Though the Church has rarely interpreted individual verses, it provides an overall understanding of Scripture through the kerygma and its corollary doctrines, roughed out by the apostles themselves (as suggested in Acts 15 and some later passages of the New Testament, such as 2 Pt 1:16-21 and 3:16), and refined by the early Fathers of the Church and the councils.

Modern scholars have alerted us to many questions about the historical accuracy of the Gospels. The Church assures us that they tell us the truth about Jesus, through both historical facts and illustrative stories, but it rarely points out which details are historical and which are symbolic. The evangelists' many disagreements over facts of minor importance make it evident that our faith in the Gospels is not founded on such factual details as the duration of Jesus' ministry (the first three evangelists imply one year, but John implies three) or the precise recording of Jesus' words. Beyond the continuing, often impossible, and sometimes enlightening effort to find Jesus' exact words and distinguish factual events from illustrative stories, lies the central reality that Christians included certain books in their canon of sacred Scripture because these books expressed their faith in Jesus as they received it through the apostolic witnesses (Lk 1:1-4). I therefore cherish the Gospel of Mark as true, usually without trying to distinguish whether certain passages are factually true of Jesus or true by way of illustrating the kind of person he was and is. For either way, the truth about Jesus leads us into personal relationship with him through prayer.

I dedicate this effort to my wife Marian, always the dearest partisan of my efforts, and to the many members of the Society of Mary who helped me appreciate the power of the Gospel.

Now, I invite you to accompany me in seeking Mark's Jesus, who, being God, is also a man just as human as we are—no, much more human, the only one who completely fulfills the human potential. Together let's muse over one image or set of images each day, letting it grow into prayer. As we begin, let's ask St. Mark to pray for us and invoke the Holy Spirit, to inspire us to find Mark's very human Jesus.

The Public Ministry of Jesus

Jesus Joins the Sinners' Line for Baptism

Mark 1:1-9: *The beginning of the good news of Jesus Christ, the Son of God... "the Lord...." John the baptizer appeared in the wilderness, proclaiming a baptism of repentance for the forgiveness of sins. And people from the whole Judean countryside...were going out to him, and were baptized by him in the river Jordan, confessing their sins....*

In those days Jesus came from Nazareth of Galilee and was baptized by John in the Jordan.

To contemplate:

Mark's first picture of Jesus looks so simple,
    and yet we sense it must be full of mystery.

Why do you come from your hills of Nazareth
    down to the Jordan to be baptized by John?
John stands there baptizing sinners;
    he tells them to cleanse their hearts in penance,
        even as he cleanses their bodies in water.

But Jesus, what do you have to do with sinners,
   you whom Mark calls the Christ,
   the Anointed One—
      the very Son of God, the Lord himself?
You whose sandals John is not worthy to remove,
   why do you join the long line of sinners,
      and wait for John to pour water on you?

It is I who should join that line of sinners.
   But you, you have no sin at all!
Why, then, do you stand there in that line?
   Do you so much want to be one of us,
      as to join us sinners?

O Jesus, how wonderful you are
   to come down from your hills of heaven
      even to our deep valley to lift us up!
How awesome that you, the very Son of God,
   became a man to be one of us,
      to suffer along with us, to feel the misery
         of being identified as a sinner.
Do you really love us that profoundly—
   to humiliate yourself to enter our line of sinners?

Jesus, I am overwhelmed by your love for me,
   carried away in silent reverie.
I picture you lining up with sinners—
   even in line with me....

Jesus, the Spirit, and the Father

Mark 1:10-11: *Just as he was coming up out of the water, he saw the heavens torn apart and the Spirit descending like a dove on him. And a voice came from heaven, "You are my Son, the Beloved; with you I am well pleased."*

To contemplate:

Mark's second picture of you, Jesus,
   portrays your intimacy with God,
      even gives us a glimpse of heaven—
         the heaven of three divine Persons.

We see the Dove—
   the Holy Spirit, Breath of the God
      of peace and love.
The Dove descends on you,
   rests on you, brings his peace to you—
      and his love.

We hear the Father,
> the voice that roared in Sinai's thunder:
>> "Keep the people back!" (Ex 19:12-24).

But here, no thunder,
> only the gentle word, "You are my Son,
>> my beloved Son!"

O Jesus, beloved Son of God himself,
> the Spirit and the Father love you
>> for identifying yourself with sinners.

The Spirit brings his peace to you;
> the Father declares his love for you,
>> in your humility his own true Son.

He has sent you to be one of us,
> to be one with me, a sinner.

You are one with the Father and the peaceful Spirit
> in the heaven above our heavens.
>> Yet you come to us, to me.

I love you for coming to me in my sinful misery.
> For now I can have hope and peace and love.

Since I am baptized into you, the Dove now
rests on me,
> and I know the Father says to me:

>> "You, too, are my beloved child!"

Jesus Is Tempted in the Wilderness

Mark 1:12-13: *And the Spirit immediately drove him out into the wilderness. He was in the wilderness forty days, tempted by Satan; and he was with the wild beasts; and the angels waited on him.*

To contemplate:

How could you, my Jesus, be tempted
   to sin as we have sinned?
How could the Spirit who guides you
   drive you into the desert of temptation?

How could the Father, who loves you,
   let you dwell with the wild beasts
      of savage fascination?

Did you feel the weakness
   of the flesh,
      demands of body
         desiring to be satisfied?
Did you know temptation
   of the mind,
      longing to know everything,
         craving to be admired?

Did you undergo temptation
   of the spirit,
      yearning to control others,
         thirsting for power, glory?

O my Jesus, you do know
   what we have felt and craved.
      You know the hunger urging us
         to snatch forbidden fruit.
You really have identified yourself
   with all of us poor sinners;
      though you've not known sin,
         you have known temptation.
Thank you for being one of us
   even in that, even in enduring
      the fascination that drives us
         to distracted frenzy.

Be with me, Jesus, when I am tempted
   to turn from the Holy Spirit
      and the loving Father....

Jesus' Good News of the Kingdom

Mark 1:14-15: *Now after John was arrested, Jesus came to Galilee, proclaiming the good news of God, and saying, "The time is fulfilled, and the kingdom of God has come near; repent, and believe in the good news."*

To contemplate:

Mark's Jesus speaks his own first word:
   "The time is *now!*"—
      the time of hope.
The time the world's been waiting for
   has finally come—
   the day Isaiah longed to see;
the great and terrible day of the Lord
   that Malachi awaited—
      great day for those who love,
   terrible for those who hate.
Day of the kingdom of God himself,
   day to repent,
      day to believe—
   the good news of the Lord.

The kingdom Daniel said would come
 to smash our world's false kingdoms (Dan 2)—
  that kingdom God now begins
 through you, Lord Jesus, *in you.*
It is the kingdom where God reigns,
 not a kingdom like those men rule,
  tyrants who aspire to power,
 trampling the rights of little ones.
It is a kingdom where men and women
 obey not other men and women—only God—
  a kingdom where no force prevails,
 but only faith and hope and love,
open to those who repent their sins,
 who let you cleanse their evil hearts—
  to those who willingly embrace
   your wonderful news, and you.

O Jesus, I say "yes" to you!
 Loose my mind and heart and will
  from all that binds me here.
Father, may thy kingdom come—
thy will be done in me.

Jesus Calls His Own

Mark 1:16-20: *As Jesus passed along the Sea of Galilee, he saw Simon and his brother Andrew casting a net into the sea—for they were fishermen. And Jesus said to them, "Follow me and I will make you fish for people." And immediately they left their nets and followed him.... He saw James...and his brother John.... Immediately he called them; and they left their father Zebedee in the boat with the hired men, and followed him.*

To contemplate:

Mark's Jesus demands all. No compromise. No strings.
    His kingdom will allow no self-serving,
        not even parent-serving.

Simon and Andrew, James and John were born to fish.
    They thought they'd catch the little fish
        of the Sea of Galilee.
But they were born to catch much greater fish,
    the men and women of Galilee
        and the whole wide world!

So they must leave the things they love so well,
   the nets and boats, their things,
   the friends they love much more—
      the hired men and their father—
         just to follow Jesus.

O Jesus, how attractive you must be
   to win them away from all they love,
   with a simple word, a flick of a finger:
      "Follow—follow me!"
And you say that word to me?
   Oh, how can I leave all that is not you,
     leave all to have only you?

You ask too much!

Unless, perhaps, I look away from things,
   even from the people I love,
     look away long enough
        to see you—only you.
And when finally I do see you
   as my very Lord,
     will I then see my things
        and the people of my life

   in the new light of your presence?

Jesus Drives Out the Unclean One

Mark 1:21-28: *They went to Capernaum; and when the sabbath came, he entered the synagogue and taught. They were astounded at his teaching, for he taught them as one having authority, and not as the scribes. Just then there was in their synagogue a man with an unclean spirit, and he cried out, "What have you to do with us, Jesus of Nazareth? Have you come to destroy us? I know who you are, the Holy One of God." But Jesus rebuked him, saying, "Be silent, and come out of him!" And the unclean spirit, convulsing him and crying with a loud voice, came out of him. They were all amazed, and they kept on asking one another, "What is this? A new teaching—with authority! He commands even the unclean spirits, and they obey him." At once his fame began to spread throughout the surrounding region of Galilee.*

To contemplate:

Mark's Jesus is strong, much too strong for demons.
Mark's Jesus is clean, too clean for unclean spirits.

Jesus, why do you demand silence of a demon
   that calls you "the Holy One of God"?
      Clearly not because you are not holy.

Because you want to be a man of mystery,
    piquing the curiosity of people
        until they see your holiness?

One word from you, and the demon's gone.
    The man who brings the kingdom of God
        can vanquish those of Satan's realm.
The witnesses are all amazed,
    Never have they seen a man
        more powerful than the devil!

Jesus, I too marvel, for I am weak.
    I too marvel at your holiness,
        for I am but dust and ashes.
When evils tyrannize my life,
    when I fail to control myself,
        and another voice than mine
            seems to speak in me,
then, Lord, cast out my evil spirit—
    speak my imprisoned spirit
        gently into freedom
            from my selfishness.

And I will turn to you, amazed,
    acclaim your power and your love of holiness.
        O Jesus, make me clean!

Jesus Cures Simon's Mother-in-Law

Mark 1:30-31: *Now Simon's mother-in-law was in bed with a fever, and they told him about her at once. He came and took her by the hand and lifted her up. Then the fever left her, and she began to serve them.*

To contemplate:

Mothers-in-law are not very popular.
    Mark's Jesus takes her by the hand,
        and that's enough to cure her.

He's come down from his own high home
    to join sinners in John's baptismal line,
    to proclaim the kingdom of God on earth,
    to attract a band of lifelong friends,
    to cast out evil unclean spirits,
        and cure a feverish mother-in-law.
He grasps her hand and helps her up.
    He stoops down to her low level
        to raise her up toward him.

He holds her wrinkled hand,
   her old hand in his young one;
      he cures her with his gentle touch.
   Kindness flows from him—into her;
      she waits on them.

O my Jesus, grasp my hand,
   my weak hand in your strong hand,
   my grasping-for-things hand
      in your loving-us hand!
My Jesus, raise me up,
   up from my feverish search for things,
   up from the ceaseless pleasure quest,
      hot pursuit of emptiness.
Raise me up to your way of life,
   up to a new love of what you love,
   up to a fresh desire to serve you
      in sick bodies and sick hearts.

My Jesus, I love you for stooping down to me;
   I love you for grasping my poor hand.
   I thank you for raising my mind
      from its bed of fevered thoughts

   to new life in you....

Jesus Works and Prays

Mark 1:32-35: *That evening, at sundown, they brought to him all who were sick or possessed with demons. And the whole city was gathered around the door. And he cured many who were sick with various diseases, and cast out many demons; and he would not permit the demons to speak, because they knew him.*

In the morning, while it was still very dark, he got up and went out to a deserted place, and there he prayed.

To contemplate:

Mark loves pictures of Jesus.
   Here he gives three striking shots:
      the people bring their sick to him;
      he cures them, casts their demons out;
      at dawn seeks God in a deserted place.

The people love him for serving all their needs
   for cures and exorcisms.
Do they love him for himself?
   For who he is, his love for them?
      Hardly, for he shuts up shouting demons,
         who try to reveal his identity
            before his people understand.

Do they know the source of his gentle love?
   The Father to whom he prays?
   The Spirit who guides his ways?
      Hardly, for he goes alone to a deserted place,
         his rendezvous with his loving Father
         and gentle Spirit of peace.

Jesus, may I find you in the crowd,
   the community of people who come to you,
   the people who need your help
      and ask for cures of body, soul.
Jesus, may I find you in the desert,
   where no one ventures but the lonely heart
   in search of God—
      loving Father and peaceful Spirit.
Jesus, may I find you as you are right now,
   at the right hand of the Father;
   in the people with whom I live.

   Father, I would speak with you,

   With your Holy Spirit, too....

Jesus Touches a Leper

Mark 1:40-45: *A leper came to him begging him, and kneeling he said to him, "If you choose, you can make me clean." Moved with pity, Jesus stretched out his hand and touched him, and said to him, "I do choose. Be made clean!" Immediately the leprosy left him, and he was made clean. After sternly warning him he sent him away at once, saying to him, "See that you say nothing to anyone; but go, show yourself to the priest, and offer for your cleansing what Moses commanded, as a testimony to them." But he went out and began to proclaim it freely, and to spread the word, so that Jesus could no longer go into a town openly, but stayed out in the country; and people came to him from every quarter.*

To contemplate:

Mark's Jesus hears our prayers,
    answers our earnest pleas.
        He wants us to request of him
            things impossible to do.

He's so deeply moved with pity,
   feels such great sympathy
      for the leper's desolation,
         he reaches out to touch him.
He touches the lonely leper!
   No one touches a leper—
      it's an easy way to *become* a leper—
         yet Jesus touches this leper!
He wills what the leper wills;
   for the leper's prayer is pure:
      "If you choose, you can make me clean.
         I know you want me clean!"
To this perfect prayer Jesus responds:
   "I choose. Be thou made clean!"
      The leprosy clears up at once;
         he stands there pure and clean.

O my Jesus, if you choose,
   you can make me clean—
      clean of all my body's ills,
         clean of all my spirit's sins.
O my Jesus, if you wish,
   you can give me strength,
      patience to control myself,
         and love to follow you.

   O my Jesus, if you choose,
      you can make me clean!

Jesus Forgives and Cures a Paralytic

Mark 2:1-12: *When he returned to Capernaum after some days, it was reported that he was at home. So many gathered around that there was no longer room for them, not even in front of the door; and he was speaking the word to them. Then some people came, bringing to him a paralyzed man, carried by four of them. And when they could not bring him to Jesus because of the crowd, they removed the roof above him; and...they let down the mat on which the paralytic lay. When Jesus saw their faith, he said to the paralytic, "Son, your sins are forgiven." Now some of the scribes were sitting there, questioning in their hearts.... "Blasphemy! Who can forgive sins but God alone?" At once Jesus...said to them..."Which is easier, to say to the paralytic, 'Your sins are forgiven,' or to say, 'Stand up and take your mat and walk'? But so that you may know that the Son of Man has authority on earth to forgive sins"—he said to the paralytic—"I say to you, stand up, take your mat and go to your home." And he stood up, and immediately took the mat and went out before all of them.*

To contemplate:

Jesus stands there, at home in Simon Peter's house,
    surrounded by a crowd so large and dense
        that four bearers of a paralytic
            can't get through to him.
So up to the roof with the motionless man they climb;
    they tear a hole in Simon Peter's roof
        and lower the paralytic,
            down in front of Jesus.

The bearers want him to cure their paralytic friend.
    But when he sees their trusting faith,
        he does an even greater thing—
            forgives his sins!
"Blasphemy!" cry the scribes in disbelieving hearts.
    But Jesus looks upon the paralytic's body,
        asks them if he proves his point
            by curing immobility.

The Son of Man stands there in Simon Peter's house,
    telling the paralytic man to stand erect.
        And he who hasn't moved for years
            twitches a hand,
then moves a foot, looks up at Jesus in wonderment
    and obediently staggers to unsteady feet;
        now straight and strong and free,
            even as his soul is free!

    O Jesus, forgive the sins that paralyze me—
        forgive me, too, O Son of Man!

Jesus Calls a Tax Collector

Mark 2:13-17: *Jesus went out again beside the sea; the whole crowd gathered around him, and he taught them. As he was walking along, he saw Levi son of Alphaeus sitting at the tax booth, and he said to him, "Follow me." And he got up and followed him.*

And as he sat at dinner in Levi's house, many tax collectors and sinners were also sitting with Jesus and his disciples—for there were many who followed him. When the scribes of the Pharisees saw that he was eating with sinners and tax collectors, they said to his disciples, "Why does he eat with tax collectors and sinners?" When Jesus heard this, he said to them, "Those who are well have no need of a physician, but those who are sick; I have come to call not the righteous but sinners."

To contemplate:

Jesus calls a tax collector
   right out of his tax booth,
then sits at the tax man's table
   to celebrate life with him.

Why would Jesus want a tax collector?
　　Nobody else wanted Levi!
　　　　They would rather see him dead,
　　squeezing the money he squeezed from them
　　　　for the domineering Romans.
Why would Jesus enter this sinner's house
　　and sit there to eat his food
　　　　and drink his wine?
　　Why lift a glass in toast to him,
　　　　relax and laugh with him?
Some scribes and Pharisees could not understand
　　how Jesus could do such things
　　　　as eat and drink with sinners.
　　They judged the man who cleansed the leper
　　　　unclean!

O Jesus, I am the one who is unclean.
　　I haven't extorted taxes,
　　　　but I've done some evil things.
　　Like Levi, I'm a sinner.
And you stop along your way to call me, too?
　　Even me, you call—
　　　　one who has understood
　　and loved so little

　　Dear Lord, I want to walk with you,
　　　　and celebrate life with you!

Jesus Is the Bridegroom

Mark 2:18-20: *Now John's disciples and the Pharisees were fasting; and people came and said to him, "Why do John's disciples and the disciples of the Pharisees fast, but your disciples do not fast?" Jesus said to them, "The wedding guests cannot fast while the bridegroom is with them, can they? As long as they have the bridegroom with them, they cannot fast. The days will come when the bridegroom is taken away from them, and then they will fast on that day."*

To contemplate:

Mark's Jesus does not fast;
   he celebrates as life's bridegroom!
When a bridegroom celebrates his marriage,
   must his wedding guests not feast?
When Jesus marries God's own people,
   how can we, his people, fast?
With the bridegroom of Isaiah's prophecy (62:5),
   Jesus identifies himself:

"For as a young man marries a woman,
  so shall your builder marry you,
and as a bridegroom takes joy in his bride,
  so shall your God rejoice in you."

Jesus and Yahweh are one!

But then the image darkens:
  the bridegroom will be taken away
(at his crucifixion and ascension)—
  then, indeed, will his people fast.

O Jesus, my beloved bridegroom,
  I love you as a bride, her husband.
  I rejoice in your loving presence.
But days pass and I forget you.
  I so feebly sense your presence.

Yet I believe that you are near,
  nearer than a bridegroom to his bride,
  nearer than a lover to his beloved!
Yes, you are near me, Lord,
  near in all your people—

> even here within me!

> And I rejoice in you!

Jesus Reveals His God

Mark 2:23-28: *One sabbath he was going through the grainfields; and as they made their way his disciples began to pluck heads of grain. The Pharisees said to him, "Look, why are they doing what is not lawful on the sabbath?" And he said to them, "Have you never read what David did when he and his companions were hungry and in need of food? He entered the house of God...and ate the bread of the Presence, which it is not lawful for any but the priests to eat, and he gave some to his companions." Then he said to them, "The sabbath was made for humankind, and not humankind for the sabbath; so the Son of Man is lord even of the sabbath."*

To contemplate:

And now Mark pictures you, my Lord,
   crossing a field with your disciples—
men so poor they garner remnants,
   as did Ruth of old.
They are poor because you, their Lord, are poor,
   and since they choose to be poor with you,
   you strongly defend their poor men's right
      to pluck the grain they need.

Some watchful Pharisees are shocked,
    angered that you allow your men
        to grind in their hands the grain from husks—
            to work on the sabbath day.
You hold up David as a prototype;
    they must accept David's authority
        to set an example of feeding his men
            with priest-reserved bread.
You know the Pharisees won't agree,
    too set against you to see your point.
        So you pronounce a deeper word,
            based on God's own action:
"God made the sabbath as his day
    of rest after six creating days.
        God made it for people to keep his rest
            so they would be free.
"This God I know, as the Son of Man—
    this God made men and women free.
    Incredibly magnanimous,
        he gives us his own day!*"*

O Son of Man, you tell us how to live all days!
    O Lord of the sabbath, God is not
    a fear-instilling God;
            for *God* is **Love** (1 Jn 4:8)!
            I love you, **Love!**

Jesus Grieves

Mark 3:1-6: *Again he entered the synagogue, and a man was there who had a withered hand. They watched him to see whether he would cure him on the sabbath, so that they might accuse him. And he said to the man who had the withered hand, "Come forward." Then he said to them, "Is it lawful to do good or to do harm on the sabbath, to save life or to kill?" But they were silent. He looked around at them with anger; he was grieved at their hardness of heart and said to the man, "Stretch out your hand." He stretched it out, and his hand was restored. The Pharisees went out and immediately conspired with the Herodians against him, how to destroy him.*

To contemplate:

Mark's Jesus accepts challenges,
   even when he knows his critics
      are watching to catch him in some "sin."
He even counter-challenges them:
   "Is it right to do good on God's day?
      What kind of God is watching us?"

Their guilty silence condemns them,
 reveals the hardness of their hearts
  that throw up legal blocks to doing good.

Jesus looks at them with anger,
 anger that they open not their hearts
  to a man with a withered hand,
   and to the man who'd cure that hand.
Jesus grieves with the grief of God (Gen 6:6),
 seeing the many
  close their hearts to him—
   hardening them as stone.
Then Jesus cures the withered hand,
 more concerned about this one poor man
  than all the harm that his enemies
   begin to plot against himself.

O Jesus, see my withered soul;
 see my own poor hardened heart.
  I grieve for closing my heart
   to some who sought to enter in.
Please heal my hardened heart,
 straighten out my withered soul.
  With mended heart I'll then reach out
   to those in greater need than I.

  Lord, heal me, heart and soul....

The Crowd Besieges Jesus

Mark 3:7-12: *Jesus departed with his disciples to the sea, and a great multitude from Galilee followed him...from Judea, Jerusalem, Idumea, beyond the Jordan, and the region around Tyre and Sidon. He told his disciples to have a boat ready for him because of the crowd, so that they would not crush him; for he had cured many, so that all who had diseases pressed upon him to touch him. Whenever the unclean spirits saw him, they fell down before him and shouted, "You are the Son of God!" But he sternly ordered them not to make him known.*

To contemplate:

He stands there by the border of the sea,
   his hair flowing with the gentle breeze;
     and a great crowd gathers,
     crushing in upon him,
   straining forward just to see him.
All the stricken press upon him,
   the jaundiced, fevered, stumbling—
     all crush in upon him,
     just to touch his body,
   hold his rough carpenter hands.

All would have a piece of him,
   all but those with unclean spirits.
     These fall before him, shout:
      "You are the Son of God!"
   Not adoring do they shout,
but in sheer fear and hate.

O Jesus, at the mercy of the crowd,
   I, too, would press in to see you,
     push and shove just to touch you,
     fall upon my knees before you,
   shouting, "You are the Son of God!"
Not in hatred would I shout,
   but in joy and love and happiness
     to be in your manly presence,
     as you stand there by the sea,
   your hair flowing in the breeze.

Hold out strong carpenter hands to me
   that I may hold fast to them,
     enfold them in my own two hands
     and bring them to my lips
   in responsive, loving kiss—

     hold you in my heart....
     Hold me in your heart!

Jesus Chooses His Twelve

Mark 3:13-19: *He went up the mountain and called to him those whom he wanted, and they came to him. And he appointed twelve, whom he also named apostles, to be with him, and to be sent out to proclaim the message, and to have authority to cast out demons. So he appointed the twelve: Simon (to whom he gave the name Peter); James son of Zebedee and John the brother of James (to whom he gave the name Boanerges, that is, Sons of Thunder); and Andrew, and Philip, and Bartholomew, and Matthew, and Thomas, and James son of Alphaeus, and Thaddaeus, and Simon the Cananaean, and Judas Iscariot, who betrayed him.*

To contemplate:

Jesus calls and they come to him,
    twelve simple men; he chooses them
to be with him for a little while,
    then go out to the whole wide world.
He has gathered them with authority,
    the authority of God himself;
he gives a share in it to them,
    to cast out demons, tell his truth.

He calls each one of them by name;
    he even gives them special names,
like "The Rock" and "The Sons of Thunder"—
    men who gave their hearts to him.
But there is one who will fail,
    will not give his heart to him,
will hold back his love—betray,
    betray the Lord who elected him!

Jesus, we know you call us, too,
    call us to live and walk with you.
And then you also send us forth,
    send us to tell the world of you.
I am afraid, dear Lord, afraid;
    I fear to live and walk with you;
like Judas, I might fail the test,
    even turn far away from you.
For the world in which I live and work
    knows little or nothing concerning you;
and what it knows it contradicts
    in word and act, in thought and deed.

Yet if you call, you give the grace
    to fulfill your beckoning.
O Lord, I pray and humbly listen,
    listen for your silent call....

Jesus' True Spirit

Mark 3:19-29: *Then he went home; and the crowd came together again, so that they could not even eat. When his family heard it, they went out to restrain him, for people were saying, "He has gone out of his mind." And the scribes...said, "He has Beelzebul, and by the ruler of the demons he casts out demons." And he called them to him, and spoke to them.... "How can Satan cast out Satan?...*

"Truly I tell you, people will be forgiven for their sins and whatever blasphemies they utter; but whoever blasphemes against the Holy Spirit can never have forgiveness, but is guilty of an eternal sin."

To contemplate:

Jesus is a man for our time, too—
   under such stress to do his work,
      he has no time to eat or rest:
         "He has gone out of his mind."
      Much worse, he is accused
of doing good by means of the evil one.

Are all those great cures of his,
> all those castings out of demons,
>> a cover for most sinister intent?
>>> Is he possessed by the demon prince?

Jesus, what an evil, twisted thought!
> You answer them with a dire warning:
>> "Who blasphemes the Holy Spirit
>>> is guilty—guilty of eternal sin!"

My Jesus, I believe the Spirit
> who dwells in you and guides your life
>> is truly the most *Holy* Spirit,
>>> opposed directly to Beelzebul.

Dear Lord, may I never oppose your Spirit,
> but welcome him to enter in.
>> Yet I still fear what he'll do in me;
>>> I fear that he will drive me hard.

They'll say of me as they said of you:
> "He has gone out of his mind!"
>> For your Spirit is a whirling wind
>>> of fire and flaming tongue.

How can I stand his force in me,
> when even you could find no rest,
>> so fierce his driving pace.

>> O Spirit, drive me hard—
>>> into the arms of Jesus!

Jesus' True Family

Mark 3:31-35: *Then his mother and his brothers came; and standing outside, they sent to him and called him. A crowd was sitting around him; and they said to him, "Your mother and your brothers and sisters are outside, asking for you." And he replied, "Who are my mother and my brothers?" And looking at those who sat around him, he said, "Here are my mother and my brothers! Whoever does the will of God is my brother and sister and mother."*

To contemplate:

Mark's Jesus looks around the room,
    looks at those he knows.
His eyes are glowing joyfully;
    he looks with eyes of love.
For they are sitting there so still,
    listening to his word.

These are the ones who listen
    in faith and hope and love,
and speak and act accordingly;
    therefore you call them *family*.

As brothers and sisters they fulfill
   your Father's future word
"This is my Beloved Son;
   listen faithfully to him" (9:7).
They carry out your Father's will:
   they listen to Beloved Son.
And so you call them *your* beloved,
   dear to you as family.

O Jesus, may I join with them,
   love you dearly as my own—
love you as Mary your mother loved,
   listening in her heart (Lk 2:51):
My Lord, "Let it be done to me
   according to your word" (Lk 1:38).

Jesus Sows Good Seed

Mark 4:1-9: *Such a very large crowd gathered around him that he got into a boat on the sea and sat there, while the whole crowd was beside the sea on the land.... "Listen! A sower went out to sow.... Some seed fell on the path, and the birds came and ate it up. Other seed fell on rocky ground, where it did not have much soil, and it sprang up quickly, since it had no depth of soil. And when the sun rose, it was scorched; and since it had no root, it withered away. Other seed fell among thorns, and the thorns grew up and choked it, and it yielded no grain. Other seed fell into good soil and brought forth grain, growing up and increasing and yielding thirty and sixty and a hundredfold." And he said, "Let anyone with ears to hear listen!"*

To contemplate:

You loved fishermen, loved their lake,
   loved gliding on it in their boats.
     So when the crowd pressed close to hear,
   you made a boat your speaker's chair.

You loved the farmers, loved their land.
    Did you seed your own small plot?
        You now have seeds of wisdom deep
    to sow among the restless crowd.
Most hear your voice but listen not;
    most seeds you sow in hearts are lost—
        plucked from the surface by Satan's birds,
        withered for lack of depth of soil,
        or choked by thorny work and care.

O Jesus, what kind of soil am I?
        Am I a path for Satan's way,
        or ground too shallow for deep root,
        or land not cleared of thorny thoughts?
    Do I, too, hear but fail to listen?
How can your word in me bear fruit
        if I trouble not to clear my heart
        of worldly weeds and thorns?
    How can your word in me bear fruit?
O Jesus, work my mind and heart!
    Plow up the weeds so rooted there,
    and with abundant watering grace
    prepare my soil to bear your word,
        grasp and love it, hold it firm—
        at last become good soil to bear
        fruit of faith and hope in you,
        fruit of love a hundredfold!
    My Jesus, I pause to listen....

Jesus Suffers Frustration

Mark 4:10-13: *When he was alone, those who were around him along with the twelve asked him about the parables. And he said to them, "To you has been given the secret of the kingdom of God, but for those outside, everything comes in parables; in order that 'they may indeed look, but not perceive, and may indeed listen, but not understand; so that they may not turn again and be forgiven.'"*

And he said to them, "Do you not understand this parable? Then how will you understand all the parables?"

To contemplate:

Mark's Jesus tells God's secrets to his own,
   but hides them from the ignorant crowd
      in parables, riddles, conundrums—
         so they won't understand.
Mark's Jesus sometimes speaks harsh words,
   the words Isaiah spoke when people
      did not hear God's word in him—
         stinging words that wound!

O Jesus, how could you really hide
 the very truth you came to tell?
  How could you deliberately
   confound your own people?
How could you really want your Father
 to withhold his great forgiving word
  from those to whom he sent you,
   crying, "Believe; repent!"?

Surely you tease us with this riddle,
 forcing us to dig into the soil
  of your word to find the seed
   you planted down so deep.
And what do we find hidden there?
 Your own so human anguished hurt,
  the wound our crass indifference
   inflicts upon your heart.

O Jesus, I know a little of that hurt;
 when others let my words fall dead,
  as I've let your words die in me!
Dear Lord, forgive my own indifference
 to the many seeds you've planted
  within my shallow mind.
 Forgive the thorns of selfishness,
  within my shallow heart.

Jesus Is Our Light

Mark 4:21-25: *He said to them, "Is a lamp brought in to be put under the bushel basket, or under the bed, and not on the lampstand? For there is nothing hidden, except to be disclosed; nor is anything secret, except to come to light. Let anyone with ears to hear listen!" And he said to them, "Pay attention to what you hear; the measure you give will be the measure you get, and still more will be given you. For to those who have, more will be given; and from those who have nothing, even what they have will be taken away."*

To contemplate:

No electric lights in Jesus' Galilee,
    no glaring signs; just little lamps of oil.
But a little lamp of oil casts light,
    marvelous light into the darkest night.

Into my own dark spiritual night,
    when meaning, beauty, goodness
        are hidden from my inner sight,
    you, Lord, cast your shining light—
        and life itself glows bright!

Ah, your light reveals not only good
   but also evil in my life,
      the little gnawing lusts
   that turn my bread to crusts,
      and stored-up treasure rusts.
Your word is light when I truly hear
   and cherish it as a guide for me,
      only when I try to heed,
   apply it to my every deed,
      let it to my life give lead.
Your light, my Lord, reveals to me
   all men and women as my kin,
      brothers and sisters mine,
   whom I must never decline
      to love, as love for you a sign.

Then you assure me that the measure
   with which I measure out my love
   will be the measure of your gifts
      for me!

O Jesus, of my life the treasure,
   light my way to give my love
   to others without measure—
      for you!

Jesus Plants God's Kingdom

Mark 4:26-33: *He also said, "The kingdom of God is as if someone would scatter seed on the ground, and would sleep and rise night and day, and the seed would sprout and grow, he does not know how. The earth produces of itself, first the stalk, then the head, then the full grain in the head. But when the grain is ripe, at once he goes in with his sickle, because the harvest has come."*

He also said, "...the kingdom of God...is like a mustard seed, which, when sown upon the ground, is the smallest of all the seeds on earth; yet when it is sown it grows up and becomes the greatest of all shrubs, and puts forth large branches, so that the birds of the air can make nests in its shade."

With many such parables he spoke the word to them, as they were able to hear it.

To contemplate:

Like Jesus we must spread God's word
   as farmers planting seeds
      of God's kingdom
         everywhere.

Like Jesus we must spread God's word
   in people's minds and hearts,
      then rest without
         anxiety.
For God is working secretly,
   giving the seed strong growth
      in minds and hearts
         he's made.
Then, at the end of life's long season
   he comes to claim the yield
      he can expect
         of us.

He plants the smallest of all the seeds,
   the seed of his kingdom Church,
      growing great branches
         for shade.
And, like birds from far and near,
   he invites us into his kingdom,
      to find at last
         our rest.

O Jesus, I grasp such simple talk;
   please open up my poor heart
      to grow in God's love
         for me.

Jesus Calms the Storm

Mark 4:35-41: *On that day, when evening had come, he said to them, "Let us go across to the other side." And leaving the crowd behind, they took him with them in the boat.... A great windstorm arose, and the waves beat into the boat, so that the boat was already being swamped. But he was in the stern, asleep on the cushion; and they woke him up and said to him, "Teacher, do you not care that we are perishing?" He woke up and rebuked the wind, and said to the sea, "Peace! Be still!" Then the wind ceased, and there was a dead calm. He said to them, "Why are you afraid? Have you still no faith?" And they were filled with great awe and said to one another, "Who then is this, that even the wind and the sea obey him?"*

To contemplate:

Is he so exhausted from his harvest work
    that even a storm will not awaken him?
So worn out, just as we at times are worn,
    that he sleeps on, even in the tossing boat?

Awakening him, they spitefully complain:
  "Don't you care, even if we die?"
And don't I sometimes think the same of him:
  "Doesn't it bother you that I am lost?"

  There he stands in the tossing boat,
    talking to the sea;
  There he stands straight and calm,
    talking to the wind.
  A madman talks to wind and sea;
    only a madman thinks
  that he can calm the raging waters
    and shrilly shrieking wind.
  Yet waves die down and screaming wind
    changes to gentle breeze.
  And he stands there calm and strong,
    master of wind and sea.
  But in this moment of divinity
    he suffers human perplexity
  that they who had seen his wondrous deeds
    could doubt he cares for them.
  Then, filled with awe, they whisper,
    "Who can this man be?"

O Jesus, fully God yet fully man,
  I come to you, human like me,
with faith and hope that in finding you
  I've found my own true God!

Jesus Casts Out "Legion"

Mark 5:1-19: *They came to...the country of the Gerasenes.... A man out of the tombs with an unclean spirit met him.... He had often been restrained with shackles and chains, but the chains he wrenched apart, and the shackles he broke in pieces; and no one had the strength to subdue him.... When he saw Jesus from a distance, he ran and bowed down before him; and he shouted at the top of his voice, "What have you to do with me?... I adjure you by God, do not torment me.... My name is Legion; for we are many.... Send us into the swine; let us enter them." So he gave them permission. And the unclean spirits came out and entered the swine; and the herd, numbering about two thousand, rushed down the steep bank into the sea, and were drowned....*

People came...to Jesus and saw the demoniac sitting there, clothed and in his right mind...and they were afraid.... They began to beg Jesus to leave.... As he was getting into the boat, the man who had been possessed by demons begged him that he might be with him. But Jesus refused, and said to him, "Go home to your friends, and tell them how much the Lord has done for you, and what mercy he has shown you."

To contemplate:

Jesus, are we sometimes like that man?
　　We come to you with "Legion" needs;
we come plagued with "Legion" thoughts
　　and cares of a world not yours.
We live among tombs of fear and death,
　　chained to a world that weighs us down.
A legion of troubles inhabit us,
　　tearing our peace of mind.

You are our only hope of peace,
　　in a world of spiraling stress and strain,
encumbered with anxieties
　　that turn our joy to dust.
Oh, send these anxious thoughts and cares
　　out of us, out of us—anywhere!
Rid us of our afflicting fears
　　at any cost, dear Lord!

Send these plagues into the swine
　　that symbolize unholy means
by which we seek unholy wealth
　　and pleasure of this world.
Only when you drown these swine
　　can our minds be truly free
to turn again to you, as *Lord*,
　　and rest our hearts in thee!

Jesus Cures a Timid Woman

Mark 5:25-34: *Now there was a woman who had been suffering from hemorrhages for twelve years. She had endured much under many physicians, and had spent all that she had; and she was no better, but rather grew worse. She had heard about Jesus, and came up behind him in the crowd and touched his cloak, for she said, "If I but touch his clothes, I will be made well." Immediately her hemorrhage stopped; and she felt in her body that she was healed of her disease.... Aware that power had gone forth from him, Jesus turned about in the crowd and said, "Who touched my clothes?" And his disciples said to him, "You see the crowd pressing in on you; how can you say, 'Who touched me?'" He looked all around to see who had done it. But the woman, knowing what had happened to her, came in fear and trembling, fell down before him, and told him the whole truth. He said to her, "Daughter, your faith has made you well; go in peace, and be healed of your disease."*

To contemplate:

Imagine Jesus in the crowd
and this suffering woman following him.

    As everyone is jostling him,
the woman, too, reaches out to him.
    But not as others does she touch:
"If I touch his clothes, I will be clean."

    She feels her body whole again,
cured of her twelve-year malady.
    But to her deep dismay he turns
and loudly asks the crowd, "Who touched me?"

    His disciples can't believe their ears:
"In such a crowd you ask who touched you?"
    Yet still he stands and looks around;
she needs yet more than body-cure.

This woman, too timid to come up front
as witness to the cure he's wrought,
    is healed in trembling spirit, too:

She kneels in faith and gratitude;
before the crowd he raises her,
    praises her faith as cause of cure.

O Jesus, I too kneel before you,
reach out to touch you with my faith,
    reach out to ask your healing love,
reach up to grasp your healing hand.

Jesus Revives a Young Girl

Mark 5:35-43: *While he was still speaking, some people came from the leader's house to say, "Your daughter is dead. Why trouble the teacher any further?" But overhearing what they said, Jesus said to the leader of the synagogue, "Do not fear, only believe...." When they came to the house of the leader of the synagogue, he saw a commotion, people weeping and wailing loudly. When he had entered, he said to them, "Why do you...weep? The child is not dead but sleeping." And they laughed at him. Then he put them all outside, and took the child's father and mother and those who were with him, and went in where the child was. He took her by the hand and said to her, "Talitha cum," which means, "Little girl, get up!" And immediately the girl got up and began to walk about (she was twelve years of age). At this they were overcome with amazement. He strictly ordered them that no one should know this, and told them to give her something to eat.*

To contemplate:

Jesus had started out to heal the leader's daughter,
   but the woman with a hemorrhage had
     delayed him,

and now the girl is dead.
No cure now—she needs her very life revived!
Completely unperturbed, he forward goes,
   scolding professional weepers, wailers,
      assuring them the girl but sleeps.
They laugh at him, deride their Lord.
He takes the girl's limp hand in his worker's hand—
   O Jesus, take my own poor hand in yours!—
      speaks to her in her native tongue,
tells her to rise up from her bed of death.

She does!

Greater than Elijah's work of raising up
   the dead son of the widow of Zarephath;
      greater than Elisha's work of raising up
   the dead son of the woman of Shunem—
      far greater than these is Jesus' work!
He loves this little girl, loves her back to life,
   orders that they give her food—
      even as he restores her life
he thinks of routine things, like food to eat.

O Jesus, Mark's and mine,
   bring me back to life again;
      sometimes my life seems dim, indeed.
Oh, make me vibrant, strong, and firm—
   my weak hand in your carpenter's hand.

Jesus Is Amazed at Nazareth's Disbelief

Mark 6:1-6: He left that place and came to his hometown, and his disciples followed him. On the sabbath he began to teach in the synagogue, and many who heard him were astounded. They said, "Where did this man get all this? What is this wisdom that has been given to him? What deeds of power are being done by his hands! Is not this the carpenter, the son of Mary and brother of James and Joses and Judas and Simon, and are not his sisters here with us?" And they took offense at him. Then Jesus said to them, "Prophets are not without honor, except in their hometown, and among their own kin, and in their own house." And he could do no deed of power there, except that he laid his hands on a few sick people and cured them. And he was amazed at their unbelief.

To contemplate:

Could Jesus truly be surprised?
   Could he feel shocked astonishment?
      If he's divine, can he be amazed?

Yet, if I deeply believe Mark's word,
  I must see the manly face of Jesus
    express astonished disbelief!
You are just as human, Mary's son,
  as I who can be surprised, amazed.
    You, too, could be astounded!
You thought you would be well received
  at Nazareth, home among your friends.
    But they wonder how you know "all this."

Everywhere else in your Galilee
  you amaze people with your power;
    but your Nazareth neighbors amaze you!
They hurt your feelings, Lord, cut deep
  into your sensitive regard for them—
    you seem inhibited from helping them.
There where you would help the most,
  you could cure only a few sick people.
    You seem a man paralyzed by hurt.
Yet something deeper lies in Mark's account—
  it is their lack of faith, their disbelief,
    that stifles your power for them.

O Jesus, you will not breach our liberty,
  our freedom to believe in you or not;
    you will not force our faith in you.
My lonely Lord, I believe in you
  and in your power to give to me
    the grace I need to live in you!

Jesus Sends Out the Twelve

Mark 6:7-13: *He called the twelve and began to send them out two by two, and gave them authority over the unclean spirits. He ordered them to take nothing for their journey except a staff; no bread, no bag, no money in their belts; but to wear sandals and not to put on two tunics. He said to them, "Wherever you enter a house, stay there until you leave the place. If any place will not welcome you and they refuse to hear you, as you leave, shake off the dust that is on your feet as a testimony against them." So they went out and proclaimed that all should repent. They cast out many demons, and anointed with oil many who were sick and cured them.*

To contemplate:

Jesus is ready to launch upon the deep;
   he widens his mission through these men,
      these fishermen he has so well prepared.
He sends them forth with nothing for their journey,
   not even bare necessities for travel—
      no bread, no bag, no money in their belts.

When I go forth to travel far and wide,
    I take my wallet, clothes, and well-packed bags;
        I go prepared, depending on myself.
And I go to satisfy, enjoy myself,
    not as missioner looking for a catch,
        not as one to spread your word, my Lord.

O Jesus, were you really so severe
    as Mark depicts you here, dedicated
        exclusively to the work of fisherman?
Your time was different, much more simple
    than our sophisticated high-tech era;
        you would be giving other orders now.

Yet I pause for thought and wonder how
    I might apply to here and now
        your stark prescriptions—
how to simplify my life and focus
    all my acts to follow you,
        be sent to do your work.

O Jesus, I am lost in thought,
    wondering what you'd have me do.
        Is it enough just to want

            to be wholly at your call?

Jesus Suffers the Stress of Action

Mark 6:16-33: *When Herod heard of it [Jesus' expanded work], he said, "John, whom I beheaded, has been raised."*

For Herod himself had...beheaded him in the prison....

The apostles gathered around Jesus, and told him all that they had done and taught. He said to them, "Come away to a deserted place all by yourselves and rest a while." For many were coming and going, and they had no leisure even to eat. And they went away in the boat to a deserted place by themselves. Now many saw them going and recognized them, and they hurried there on foot from all the towns and arrived ahead of them.

To contemplate:

John beheaded!
  Mark gives details too gruesome for our educated
  palates—
    no, just right for a modern movie
  with plotting Herodias, dancing Salome,
  drunken Herod,
    and the head of John the Baptist
      on a platter!

Soon after Herod kills the Baptist, he hears
of Jesus working wonders,
> sending out disciples on new quests.
> Soon after Herod kills the preacher he so feared,
>> John seems back upon the scene
>>> to plague him.

No, a greater than John has come, a new king of
Herod's people;
> yet one who will, like John, be murdered
>> for his truth.

Meanwhile, this leader gathers those he taught
and sent to teach.
> But there's no rest for him or for his men,
>> no time to eat or plan escape
>>> from pressing mob.

> O Jesus, did you know the stress,
>> anxiety that we endure today?
> No time to eat or rest or sleep—
>> our lives are swallowed up in act;
> we cannot even think or pray.

> Jesus, you felt the stress we feel,
>> the hurrying press of action.
> You too were pushed and pulled apart.
>> I accept this life—embrace
> my share of blessed life with you!

Jesus Feeds the Hungry

Mark 6:34-44: *He saw a great crowd; and he had compassion for them...like sheep without a shepherd; and he began to teach them many things. When it grew late, his disciples came to him and said, "This is a deserted place, and the hour is now very late; send them away so that they may go into the surrounding country and villages and buy something for themselves to eat." But he answered them, "You give them something to eat." They said to him, "Are we to go and buy two hundred denarii worth of bread, and give it to them to eat?" And he said to them, "How many loaves have you?..." "Five, and two fish." Then he ordered them to get all the people to sit down in groups on the green grass. So they sat down in groups of hundreds and of fifties. Taking the five loaves and the two fish, he looked up to heaven, and blessed and broke the loaves, and gave them to his disciples to set before the people; and he divided the two fish among them all. And all ate and were filled; and they took up twelve baskets full of broken pieces and of the fish. Those who had eaten the loaves numbered five thousand men.*

To contemplate:

Jesus feels compassion for the people,
  like poor sheep abandoned by their shepherd.
Good shepherds lead their sheep to grazing fields,
  but Jesus leads them to a deserted place—
so busy feeding them with teachings wise,
  he has forgotten their bodies' basic needs.

His disciples bring him back again to earth—
  these people are in need of body-food.
But Jesus will not take the easy way
  of sending them to towns to buy their food.
Aghast, his disciples gasp, "The cost to us—
  two hundred days of work to feed this crowd—
we have but two fish and five loaves of bread!"
  Yet the impractical master commands:
"Distribute the five loaves and the two fish
  to the five thousand families standing there!"

Picture the miraculous distribution!

O Jesus, you can do it for you really know
  where bread and fish come from—
    your heavenly Father.

You can do it for you have the divine power
  to bless with your human hands
    and give to us.

  I, too, am hungry for your food....

Jesus Saves His Disciples from Drowning

Mark 6:45-52: *Immediately he made his disciples get into the boat and go on ahead to the other side, to Bethsaida, while he dismissed the crowd. After saying farewell to them, he went up on the mountain to pray.*

When evening came, the boat was out on the sea, and he was alone on the land. When he saw that they were straining at the oars against an adverse wind, he came towards them early in the morning, walking on the sea. He intended to pass them by. But when they saw him walking on the sea, they thought it was a ghost and cried out; for they all saw him and were terrified. But immediately he spoke to them and said, "Take heart, it is I; do not be afraid." Then he got into the boat with them and the wind ceased. And they were utterly astounded, for they did not understand about the loaves, but their hearts were hardened.

To contemplate:

Mark shows us Jesus on the mountaintop,
    praying to his Father.

He looks up as he feels a strong wind,
   and strains to see his straining twelve,
      fighting wind and wave.

My Jesus, now upon your mountaintop—
   your throne in heaven far above—
are you aware of winds that howl at us
   and waves that fiercely batter us?
And when we feel the danger of dread night,
   closing upon us threateningly,
will you come walking on our raging sea
   to save and comfort us?

Why did you mean to pass them by?
   Were you recalling to their minds
the far-off time when Yahweh answered
   Moses' prayer to see his glory:
"In my goodness I will pass before you" (Ex 33:19)?
   Only Yahweh walks upon the sea (Job 9:8),
but they see *you* walk upon the sea!
   And all of them are filled with fear,
until you climb aboard their boat,
   and calm both wind and wave.

O Jesus, when wild wind and mounting wave
   threaten my fragile life;
      when all seems lost,
         come into my throbbing heart,
      and calm my sea!

Jesus Heals All Who Touch Him

Mark 6:53-56: *When they had crossed over, they came to land at Gennesaret and moored the boat. When they got out of the boat, people at once recognized him, and rushed about that whole region and began to bring the sick on mats to wherever they heard he was. And wherever he went, into villages or cities or farms, they laid the sick in the marketplaces, and begged him that they might touch even the fringe of his cloak; and all who touched it were healed.*

To contemplate:

Mark's Jesus
walks through farms and towns,
   healing all the sick—
healing all who reach down to touch
   the fringe reminding him
to be holy to the Lord (Num 15:38-40).

   The people rush
to gather all the sick
   for his healing touch.

And as he passes on his way,
   they reach out to him,
touch the fringe of his cloak.
   They touch him—
touch this Lord of life
   and are made whole!

   Lord, heal my heart
of all its waywardness;
   heal my mind
of all its fickleness;
   heal my body
of all its weaknesses;
   heal my soul
of all its sinfulness.

   Let me touch
the fringe of your holiness;
   let me feel
the edge of your gentleness;
   let me see
the tassel of your tenderness;
   let me hear
the voice of your forgiveness;
   let me taste
      the sweetness of your Eucharist.

Jesus Calls for Goodness of Heart

Mark 7:5-23: *The Pharisees and the scribes asked him, "Why do your disciples not live according to the tradition of the elders, but eat with defiled hands?" He said to them, "Isaiah prophesied rightly about you hypocrites, as it is written,*

'This people honors me with their lips,

but their hearts are far from me;

in vain do they worship me, teaching human precepts as doctrines.'

You abandon the commandment of God and hold to human tradition...."

He said to [his disciples]..."Do you not see that whatever goes into a person from outside cannot defile, since it enters, not the heart but the stomach, and goes out into the sewer?" (Thus he declared all foods clean.) And he said, "It is what comes out of a person that defiles. For it is from within, from the human heart, that evil intentions come: fornication, theft, murder, adultery, avarice, wickedness, deceit, licentiousness, envy, slander, pride, folly. All these evil things come from within, and they defile a person."

To contemplate:

Mark's Jesus is outspoken,
>not afraid to talk about a sewer.
>>He uses physical facts of life
>to teach deep spiritual truths.

Jesus pointed out the deeper reasons
>behind observance of the law
>>and uncovered the shallowness
>of observance for its own sake.

You, my Lord,
>knew the heart of your Father.
>>The holiness you call for, Lord,
>is holiness of heart.

O Jesus, strong Lord of strong hearts,
>form my weak heart like yours,
>>to love all that you have loved,
>to hate all that you have hated,
and hold with everlasting strength
>all you've taught and all you've done.
>>I listen in my heart....

Jesus Hears a Woman's Humble Prayer

Mark 7:25-30: *A woman whose little daughter had an unclean spirit...came and bowed down at his feet. Now the woman was a Gentile, of Syrophoenician origin. She begged him to cast the demon out of her daughter. He said to her, "Let the children be fed first, for it is not fair to take the children's food and throw it to the dogs." But she answered him, "Sir, even the dogs under the table eat the children's crumbs." Then he said to her, "For saying that, you may go—the demon has left your daughter." So she went home, found the child lying on the bed, and the demon gone.*

To contemplate:

Mark's Jesus sometimes seems so insensitive.
   Before he heals her daughter,
      he tests this woman's faith.

But when I look again,
   I see something beneath Mark's line—
      Jesus prepares this woman
         to receive a miracle.

Perhaps she's been too forward, daring
  to beg a favor only Jews might ask
    as God's own chosen children.
      She must know her place.

Oh, all too human thought!
  Would Mark have us see his Lord
    so human as to suffer bias,
      the bias that stains us?
Or is Mark suggesting that his Lord
  sees into a heart of faith enough
    to humbly withstand trial?
      She asks for scraps!

O Jesus, generous, loving Lord,
  you give her more than scraps—
    you give her daughter back,
      safe from demon's grasp!
The faith you ask of us, dear Lord,
  is humble faith that loves
    even when it seems rebuffed—
      faith of humble heart.
    Give me such faith, my Lord!

Jesus Heals a Deaf-Mute

Mark 7:32-37: *They brought to him a deaf man who had an impediment in his speech; and they begged him to lay his hand on him. He took him aside in private, away from the crowd, and put his fingers into his ears, and he spat and touched his tongue. Then looking up to heaven, he sighed and said to him, "Ephphatha," that is, "Be opened." And immediately his ears were opened, his tongue was released, and he spoke plainly. Then Jesus ordered them to tell no one; but the more he ordered them, the more zealously they proclaimed it. They were astounded beyond measure, saying, "He has done everything well; he even makes the deaf to hear and the mute to speak."*

To contemplate:

Jesus takes the afflicted man aside
    from all the others; just the man
        and Jesus, alone together.
But Mark's Jesus seems again so crude,
    poking fingers into his ears,
        touching his tongue with spit.

Then sighing to heaven, Jesus commands
   "Be opened!"—and his ears can hear!
      His tongue can plainly speak!

Those who hear the healed man tell
   what Jesus did for him, exclaim:
      "He has done all things well;
         he makes the deaf to hear,
            the mute to speak."
Don't we often say, "Appearances deceive"?
   How true of these appearances!
      Jesus gives a man who cannot hear
         signs of what he's doing—
            giving of himself.

Jesus gives him a share in his own hearing,
   a share in his own speaking,
   a share in his own living.
O Jesus, I too am deaf and dumb!
   I cannot hear the voice of God,
      or speak my heart to him.
My Lord, give me a share in your very self,
   to hear God's word as you hear it,
      speak to him as you speak—
         to God as Father,
            my Father,
            Our Father....

Jesus Feeds the Gentiles

Mark 7:31—8:9: *In the region of the Decapolis [ten Gentile cities]...when there was again a great crowd without anything to eat, he called his disciples and said to them, "I have compassion for the crowd, because they have been with me now for three days and have nothing to eat. If I send them away hungry to their homes, they will faint on the way—and some of them have come from a great distance.... How many loaves do you have?" They said, "Seven." Then he ordered the crowd to sit down on the ground; and he took the seven loaves, and after giving thanks he broke them and gave them to his disciples to distribute; and they distributed them to the crowd. They had also a few small fish; and after blessing them, he ordered that these too should be distributed. They ate and were filled; and they took up the broken pieces left over, seven baskets full. Now there were about four thousand people.*

To contemplate:

Again Mark's Jesus feeds the crowd,
  this time of Gentile people.
Lord, you love us all—no bias
  favoring race or creed.
You feed us all, each one of us,
  with the bounty of God's earth.

You take the loaves in your pure hands,
  seven loaves, like seven gifts
    your Spirit will later give.
You thank the Father for these gifts,
  then break them into portions
    your disciples then dispense.

Foreshadowing of your Eucharist!
  Today you still feed us bread.
But instead of simple bread and fish,
  your own body and blood you give,
transforming us from aimless crowd
  to community in you.

One in you!

Lord Jesus, our Jesus,
  feed our bodies, feed our souls;
    we long to be your own,
  to live the life you live!

My Jesus, our Jesus,
feed our bodies;
  feed our souls....

Jesus Warns of False Teachers

Mark 8:11-21: *The Pharisees came…asking him for a sign from heaven, to test him. And he sighed deeply in his spirit and said, "Why does this generation ask for a sign? Truly I tell you, no sign will be given to this generation…." And getting into the boat again, he went across to the other side.*

Now the disciples had forgotten to bring any bread; and they had only one loaf with them in the boat. And he cautioned them, saying, "Watch out—beware of the yeast of the Pharisees and the yeast of Herod." They said to one another, "It is because we have no bread." And becoming aware of it, Jesus said to them, "Why are you talking about having no bread?… Do you have eyes, and fail to see? Do you have ears, and fail to hear?… When I broke the five loaves for the five thousand, how many baskets full of broken pieces did you collect?" They said to him, "Twelve." "And the seven for the four thousand, how many baskets full of broken pieces did you collect?" And they said to him, "Seven." Then he said to them, "Do you not yet understand?"

To contemplate:

Nobody understands you, Jesus—
   the Pharisees fail to understand
      the meaning of your multiplying
         bread and fish to feed the people
           they leave hungry.
Nobody understands you, Jesus—
   not even your disciples understand
      your warning to beware of those Pharisees
         who teach false doctrines
           to hungering people.
Not even your own disciples
   grasp the inner meaning of your acts,
      the signs of power you have given,
         power to feed your people,
           satisfy their hunger.

O Jesus, lonely Jesus...
   No one understands—
      even now we fail to understand
         what you have said and done.
You exhausted yourself in preaching,
   consumed your energy in working
      miracle after marvelous miracle;
         yet we see but the outer shell.
We are so literal, so superficial, Lord.
   Show us the inner meaning
      of your life for us—
         your life in us!

Jesus Heals the Blind

Mark 8:22-26: *They came to Bethsaida. Some people brought a blind man to him and begged him to touch him. He took the blind man by the hand and led him out of the village; and when he had put saliva on his eyes and laid his hands on him, he asked him, "Can you see anything?" And the man looked up and said, "I can see people, but they look like trees, walking." Then Jesus laid his hands on his eyes again; and he looked intently and his sight was restored, and he saw everything clearly. Then he sent him away to his home, saying, "Do not even go into the village."*

To contemplate:

Mark's Jesus has just refused those who ask
   a special sign that he speaks for God.
He has just rebuked dull-witted disciples
   for remaining deaf after hearing
     the deaf and dumb man speak,
   for being blind to all he's done
     for them and for his people.

Once more he works to open their eyes:
   he cures a blind man, gives new sight
      to one who doesn't ask.
For others asked this cure with faith
   enough for him to act,
      enough to start the cure.
He gives the man a sign upon his eyes,
   a sign he'll wash them clean,
      that he may see again.

He sees...but only vaguely—
   confuses people with trees;
      weak faith needs time.
Jesus gives him time to grow in faith,
   then touches his eyes once more—
      and he sees perfectly!

O Jesus, just as you gave this man
   a second chance to see,
      just as you gave your twelve
      a second chance to see,
   give me a second chance, a third.
For my blindness and my deafness are profound—
   I am blind and deaf in spirit.

   I grope for you, my Lord....

You Are the Messiah

Mark 8:27-30: *Jesus went on with his disciples to the villages of Caesarea Philippi; and on the way he asked his disciples, "Who do people say that I am?" And they answered him, "John the Baptist; and others, Elijah; and still others, one of the prophets." He asked them, "But who do you say that I am?" Peter answered him, "You are the Messiah." And he sternly ordered them not to tell anyone about him.*

To contemplate:

As Jesus walks along a pagan road,
   he asks his disciples who he is.
He has spent his time and strength to demonstrate,
   has healed the deaf and cured the blind.
And finally they have really *heard and seen him*
   through his caring words and acts.

At last they've caught a fleeting glimpse
   of divinity in him.
Impulsive Peter speaks for all:
   "You are truly the Messiah."

Messiah means "Anointed One"!
 What, then, did Peter mean?

Did he mean the man who would be king,
 anointed king in David's line,
  Israel's greatest king?
To David, the prophet Nathan pledged:
 "God will raise your offspring up,
  firmly fix his kingdom....
 God will establish your heir's throne
  forever and forever" (2 Sam 7:12-13).
And that is what the Psalmist sang:
 "The Lord God says to David's lord,
  'Sit here at my right hand
 until I make your enemies
  your footstool'" (Ps 110:1).

O Jesus, be my anointed king forever,
 my king sitting at the right hand
  of the Lord God, your Father.
 My king, yourself the Lord—
  my Lord forever!

Jesus, along with Peter, I believe in you,
 my Anointed One, my Christ!

Jesus Must Suffer

Mark 8:31-33: *Then he began to teach them that the Son of Man must undergo great suffering, and be rejected by the elders, the chief priests, and the scribes, and be killed, and after three days rise again. He said all this quite openly. And Peter took him aside and began to rebuke him. But turning and looking at his disciples, he rebuked Peter and said, "Get behind me, Satan! For you are setting your mind not on divine things but on human things."*

To contemplate:

Jesus, *Son of Man,* has just received
   Peter's testimony of faith—
      faith that Jesus is the Messiah,
   the Anointed One,
      who will save us, his sinful people.
Yet the Son of Man rebukes poor Peter
   with the harshest name of all:
      "You Satan!"
   Peter is a tempter who would block
      Jesus' way to death.

Jesus has a plan he must fulfill,
   a mission his Father's given him—
      a sacrifice!
   Instead of the foundation rock (Mt 16:18),
      Peter's become a stumbling block.
Yes, Jesus is the great Messiah,
   but not as Peter thinks.
      For not as humans think
      does God, his Father, plan
      the future of his Son!
God's plan runs infinitely deep,
   deeper than human thought,
      deeper than Satan's plan.
   Jesus must suffer in extreme,
      be rejected, even killed—
   killed for being the Son of God
      who teaches his Father's love;
   killed for being the Son of Man
      who saves us from our sins.

O Jesus, much less than Simon Peter
   we understand God's grand design.
      Why must you suffer so and die?
      Why must we all suffer and die?
Jesus, we listen, for your reply....

Take Up Your Cross!

Mark 8:34-9:1: *He called the crowd with his disciples, and said to them, "If any want to become my followers, let them deny themselves and take up their cross and follow me. For those who want to save their life will lose it, and those who lose their life for my sake, and for the sake of the gospel, will save it. For what will it profit them to gain the whole world and forfeit their life? Indeed, what can they give in return for their life? Those who are ashamed of me and of my words in this adulterous and sinful generation, of them the Son of Man will also be ashamed when he comes in the glory of his Father with the holy angels.... Truly I tell you, there are some standing here who will not taste death until they see that the kingdom of God has come with power."*

To contemplate:

It is too much—that you should suffer, Lord!
    And why must we, too, suffer so?
        What's left to expiate
           after your cross?

What is it in my cross that is so priceless?
   Why deny myself the good things
      this world offers me—
         delicious joys?

Why so high a price to walk with you?
   Why give up my life, God's gift,
      his birthday gift to me—
         precious life?
I'm not anxious to gain the whole world,
   I rest content with my little piece.
      Must I give up even
         my little piece?

But as I read again these lines of Mark
   I think I see a gleam of light:
      not life must I give up,
         but living death.
For this life I now possess ends in death
   if I cling to it, disbelieving
      your promise of new life,
         eternal life!

If, for you, I loosely hold my present life
   and reach up for that eternal life
      with you and with our Father,
         you will save me!
   O Jesus, I reach up—save me!

Jesus Transfigured

Mark 9:2-8: *Six days later, Jesus took with him Peter and James and John, and led them up a high mountain apart, by themselves. And he was transfigured before them, and his clothes became dazzling white, such as no one on earth could bleach them. And there appeared to them Elijah with Moses, who were talking with Jesus. Then Peter said to Jesus, "Rabbi, it is good for us to be here; let us make three dwellings, one for you, one for Moses, and one for Elijah." He did not know what to say, for they were terrified. Then a cloud overshadowed them, and from the cloud there came a voice, "This is my Son, the Beloved; listen to him!" Suddenly when they looked around, they saw no one with them any more, but only Jesus.*

To contemplate:

There he stands on the mountaintop,
   his clothes shining dazzling white,
     his face brighter than the sun,
         his whole being translucent.

He stands apart from all the world,
   above this world of space and time;
      past and future, present to him—
         ancients at his beckoning.

Men long dead now speak with him:
   Moses, mediator of Sinai's laws,
      Elijah, most heroic prophet
         in young Israel's promised land.
What now does Jesus say to them?
   And what do ancients say to him?
      Does he often speak to men of old
         in talk beyond imagining?

Stunned, Peter tries to add his bit.
   He wants to make this moment last
      by building shrines for their return
         to glimpse again such heaven.
But the cloud of presence interrupts.
   A greater voice than ancients' speaks,
      the Ancient One himself commands:
         "Listen to my beloved Son!"
As quickly as glory shines, it fades.
   Elijah and Moses disappear;
      silent is the Father's voice.
         Cloud gone, only Jesus there.

O Jesus, you alone, enough for me!
To you I listen, God's beloved Son....

Coming Down the Mountain

Mark 9:9-13: *As they were coming down the mountain, he ordered them to tell no one about what they had seen, until after the Son of Man had risen from the dead. So they kept the matter to themselves, questioning what this rising from the dead could mean. Then they asked him, "Why do the scribes say that Elijah must come first?" He said to them, "Elijah is indeed coming first to restore all things. How then is it written about the Son of Man, that he is to go through many sufferings and be treated with contempt? But I tell you that Elijah has come, and they did to him whatever they pleased, as it is written about him."*

To contemplate:

Coming down the mountainside with Jesus,
   we listen as the Father has commanded.
      But what is he really saying
         that we can understand?
Jesus tells Peter and James and John
   to guard in silence what they've seen,
      until the time comes to witness
         his rising from the dead.

But none has ever risen from the dead—
  neither Moses nor Elijah have done that!
    So what could he ever mean by talk
      of rising from the dead?

Does he mean the end of all the world—
  the prophets' awesome day of the Lord?
    "Why, then, do scribes still say
    Elijah must return before that day?
      Where is Elijah now?"
"Yes, an Elijah must prepare the way;
  he came, has baptized in the Jordan.
    If that prophecy's been fulfilled,
    why not the prophecies that say
      the Son of Man must suffer?

"For John the Baptist, with Elijah's fire,
  has suffered violent, oh so violent death!
    Will not, then, the Son of Man himself
      suffer, oh so violent death?"
Jesus, as you prepared your three disciples,
  prepare me, too, to understand your death
    and enter into the suffering and death
      that I, as human, must endure—
      that I, as Christian, can endure
        only with you!

Jesus Heals a Raving Boy

Mark 9:15-29: *When the whole crowd saw him, they were immediately overcome with awe.... "Teacher, I brought you my son; he has a spirit that makes him unable to speak; and whenever it seizes him, it dashes him down; and he foams and grinds his teeth and becomes rigid; and I asked your disciples to cast it out, but they could not do so." He answered them, "You faithless generation, how much longer must I be among you? How much longer must I put up with you? Bring him to me...." When the spirit saw him, immediately it convulsed the boy, and he fell on the ground and rolled about, foaming at the mouth. Jesus asked the father, "How long has this been happening to him?" And he said, "From childhood. It has often cast him into the fire and into the water, to destroy him; but if you are able to do anything, have pity on us and help us." Jesus said to him, "If you are able!—All things can be done for the one who believes." Immediately the father of the child cried out, "I believe; help my unbelief!"...[Jesus] rebuked the unclean spirit, saying to it, "You spirit that keeps this boy from speaking and hearing, I command you, come out of him, and never enter him again!" After crying out and convulsing him terribly, it came out, and the boy was like a corpse, so that most of them said, "He*

is dead." *But Jesus took him by the hand and lifted him up, and he was able to stand. When he had entered the house, his disciples asked him privately, "Why could we not cast it out?" He said to them, "This kind can come out only through prayer."*

To contemplate:

Down from the mount of transfiguration,
   down to earthy reality once more—
      ugly scene of helpless disciples,
         curious crowd and raging demon.

He who talked with the ancient ones
   now encounters this petty failure
      of those he'd left behind to heal
         earth's petty problems, giant flaws!

He's disappointed, angry, outraged:
   "How long," he cries, "how long endure
      the blind and helpless pettiness
         of disciples without faith!"
(O Jesus, can you say those words of me?)

He even loses patience with the father
   who begs him to heal his poor distracted son.
      But when that father pleads for faith,
         he gives him faith—then cures his son.

O Jesus, I, too, pray for greater faith.
   I, too, pray for healing of my soul—
      and the precious gift of prayer....

They Will Kill Him, But He Will Rise Again

Mark 9:30-32: *They went on from there and passed through Galilee. He did not want anyone to know it; for he was teaching his disciples, saying to them, "The Son of Man is to be betrayed into human hands, and they will kill him, and three days after being killed, he will rise again." But they did not understand what he was saying and were afraid to ask him.*

To contemplate:

Let's walk along with him through Galilee,
    watching his every step,
        hearing his every word.
As we watch his steady step toward death,
    we wonder why he now avoids
        the crowds that worship him.

We hear him call himself the Son of Man
    who must endure betrayal
        "into human hands"—
            cruel hands that kill.

He knows he's walking to his death;
  yet he walks on through Galilee.
    And we are wondering
      if we'll die with him!

But death is not his final word;
  he says he'll rise again!
    Rise in being not forgotten,
      remembered by his twelve?
Rise as spirit, ghost or phantom,
  haunting those who killed him?
    Rise as ghost to haunt
      disciples who lack faith
        to die with him?
Rise in the body we now see?
  Rise with his life restored
    to walk on roads of Galilee?

Or will he rise into some new life,
  like that of glory on the mount
    when he talked with ancient ones?

O Jesus, let me walk through life with you.
  Let me unite my pain with yours—
    even die with you,
      to rise with you!

A Child in Jesus' Arms

Mark 9:33-37: *Then they came to Capernaum; and when he was in the house he asked them, "What were you arguing about on the way?" But they were silent, for on the way they had argued with one another who was the greatest. He sat down, called the twelve, and said to them, "Whoever wants to be first must be last of all and servant of all." Then he took a little child and put it among them; and taking it in his arms, he said to them, "Whoever welcomes one such child in my name welcomes me, and whoever welcomes me welcomes not me but the one who sent me."*

To contemplate:

If Jesus is marching to his death,
   who will take his place
      as first among them?
   Who will then be greatest?
Will he explode again in anger?
   Will he cry again, "How long?"
      They give him greater cause
   for outburst than before.

But he sits down among the twelve
   and simply says the greatest
      must become the servant,
   humble servant of the rest.
He demonstrates with a child;
   a little child he takes in his arms.
      See Jesus, gentle Lord,
   embrace this little child!

O Jesus, take me in your arms,
   your gentle, loving arms;
      as you received this child,
   wrap shielding arms 'round me!
Ah, you lay down one condition—
   I must first reach out my arms,
      receive such a little child
   into my own gentle arms.
Jesus, Mark's sometimes angry Lord,
   I picture your kind face,
      your bending toward a child,
   to hold it in loving arms.
I want to be this same small child,
   the one you chose to hold
      close to your beating heart
   in strong carpenter arms.
   Hold me close, my Lord!

One Cup of Water

Mark 9:38-41: *John said to him, "Teacher, we saw someone casting out demons in your name, and we tried to stop him, because he was not following us." But Jesus said, "Do not stop him; for no one who does a deed of power in my name will be able soon afterward to speak evil of me. Whoever is not against us is for us. For truly I tell you, whoever gives you a cup of water to drink because you bear the name of Christ will by no means lose the reward."*

To contemplate:

Jesus called John and James "Boanerges—
   sons of thunder."
And here John shows the name is right—
   he loves to thunder!

But Jesus himself is not a thunderer;
   he does not stop the user of his name
      from expelling demons.
Instead, he shows again his clemency:
   "Whoever's not against us is surely for us"—
      kind-hearted judgment!

He caps his lesson with a striking pledge:
"One cup of water in the name of Christ,
I will reward."

Lord, did you really call yourself "the Christ"?
Or does Mark slip in his Easter faith in you
to make his point?
Does it matter which, if here he declares his faith
that Peter had it right when he acclaimed you
as our Messiah?
We too believe you watch—but not as Boanerges—
you watch to see us do one kindly act
and bless our love.

For such an act calls strongly to your heart,
the heart that spends itself in constant service
to all others.
Jesus, our Lord who governs us by serving;
teach us to love and serve our brothers, sisters,
as you serve us.
We watch you, Jesus, serve your chosen ones
the precious water of your kindly word—
your word of life.

And we listen to our Christ....

Be Salted with Fire

Mark 9:42-50: *"If any of you put a stumbling block before one of these little ones who believe in me, it would be better for you if a great millstone were hung around your neck and you were thrown into the sea. If your hand causes you to stumble, cut it off; it is better for you to enter life maimed than to have two hands and to go to hell, to the unquenchable fire. And if your foot causes you to stumble, cut it off; it is better for you to enter life lame than to have two feet and to be thrown into hell. And if your eye causes you to stumble, tear it out; it is better for you to enter the kingdom of God with one eye than to have two eyes and to be thrown into hell, where their worm never dies, and the fire is never quenched.*

"For everyone will be salted with fire. Salt is good; but if salt has lost its saltiness, how can you season it? Have salt in yourselves, and be at peace with one another."

To contemplate:

When Peter, Rock, set himself as a stumbling block
  to turn Jesus from his Father's mission,
    Jesus called him Satan, evil one.

Now Jesus warns that anyone who blocks the path
   of little, humble ones from faith in him,
      will suffer Satan's fiery fate.
So tenderly does Jesus love the little ones,
   he has harsh words for the "greater" one
      who'd mislead them from his way.
The one who leads astray these little ones
   will strongly wish he'd never lived:
      "Better that a grinding stone
      sink him deep into the sea!
If your foot makes you stumble, cut it off!
   If your eye leads you into sin, tear it out!"
      Strong figures of the self-control
      he calls us to apply!

The disciples have been arguing
   about who of them is greatest,
   spoiling the covenant salt (Lev 2:13).
But salt to improve the taste of food
   and cauterize new wounds—
   salt is a cleansing fire
   that all must undergo.

Lord Jesus, purify our friendships,
   even though it stings
   like cauterizing salt
   to cure us of our wounds.

What God Has Joined

Mark 10:2-12: *Some Pharisees came, and to test him they asked, "Is it lawful for a man to divorce his wife?" He answered them, "What did Moses command you?" They said, "Moses allowed a man to write a certificate of dismissal and to divorce her." But Jesus said to them, "Because of your hardness of heart he wrote this commandment for you. But from the beginning of creation, 'God made them male and female. For this reason a man shall leave his father and mother and be joined to his wife, and the two shall become one flesh.' So they are no longer two, but one flesh. Therefore what God has joined together, let no one separate."*

Then in the house the disciples asked him again about this matter. He said to them, "Whoever divorces his wife and marries another commits adultery against her; and if she divorces her husband and marries another, she commits adultery."

To contemplate:

What thinks unmarried Jesus of divorce?
 Will he look to the teaching of Shammai,

allowing divorce only
    for unfaithfulness;
or to that of the rabbi Hillel,
    granting divorce for lesser causes?
"And Moses," he asks, "what did Moses say?"
    "Yes, great Moses, too, allowed divorce."
Jesus looks down deep within their hearts
    to break a way for God to enter in,
reminds them God made sex, made male and female
    for one another, one single flesh—together.
It's God himself who joins the wedding pair:
    "What therefore God himself has joined together,
let no human power presume to separate!"
    No bride or groom can break their holy bond;
no religion, tribe, or nation can undo it.
    Marriage is a sacred bond, a covenant
like God's own covenant
    with his chosen people.
To break with spouse is to break a covenant.
    Can human beings sanction such a break?

Son of God, you alone can speak for God:
    "Whoever divorces spouse and marries another
commits adultery, a breach of faithfulness.
    Whoever loves his wife, loves God her Maker."
Father, thanks for the spouse you gave to me!

Let Little Children Come to Me

Mark 10:13-16: *People were bringing little children to him in order that he might touch them; and the disciples spoke sternly to them. But when Jesus saw this, he was indignant and said to them, "Let the little children come to me; do not stop them; for it is to such as these that the kingdom of God belongs. Truly I tell you, whoever does not receive the kingdom of God as a little child will never enter it." And he took them up in his arms, laid his hands on them, and blessed them.*

To contemplate:

A graphic scene of people
   with their little ones
      who long for touch—
         Jesus' touch.
But his protective band
   would guard him from them:
      "Keep your distance.
         Stay away."

Then Jesus grows indignant—
　　not at parents or their tots,
　　　　but at disciples,
　　　　　　unenlightened.
"Let little children come to me—
　　I will receive them all,
　　　　embrace them all,
　　　　　　bless each one."

He uses this so simple scene
　　to show his Father's plan—
　　　　of such as these,
　　　　　　God's kingdom.
And only little ones like these
　　can enter it, enter life;
　　　　only little ones
　　　　　　live eternally!

O Jesus, just as you embraced
　　small children in strong arms;
　　　　as you hugged them,
　　　　　　oh, do hug me!
Yet first, I know what I must do:
　　be simple like these little ones.
　　　　I ask you, then,
　　　　make me a little child.

Where Is Your Treasure?

Mark 10:17-22: *A man ran up and knelt before him, and asked him, "Good Teacher, what must I do to inherit eternal life?" Jesus said to him, "Why do you call me good? No one is good but God alone. You know the commandments: 'You shall not murder; You shall not commit adultery; You shall not steal; You shall not bear false witness; You shall not defraud; Honor your father and mother.'" He said to him, "Teacher, I have kept all these since my youth." Jesus, looking at him, loved him and said, "You lack one thing; go, sell what you own, and give the money to the poor, and you will have treasure in heaven; then come, follow me." When he heard this, he was shocked and went away grieving, for he had many possessions.*

To contemplate:

Jesus, why not let the rich man
    call you *"Good* teacher"?
"No one is good but God alone"—
    but aren't you God himself?

You let the woman with the hemorrhage
   and the Syrophoenician woman
fall down before your feet.
   Why object to this rich man?

Must you suffer first and even die
   before he'll understand?
Must he see you first as fully man
   before he'll know you're God?
And why are you not satisfied
   with a man who keeps God's law?
How is he lacking anything
   after keeping God's commands?

When he says he has been true to God,
   Mark tells us that you love him.
Why would he have to do yet more,
   if you already love him?
"Sell all you have, give to the poor;
   then come and follow me."
O Jesus, do you demand so much
   of those who would be yours?

Your very love expects of us
   much more than we can give.
Then love us ever more and more,
   that we find more to give—

   your own eternal love!

Only God Can Save

Mark 10:23-31: *Then Jesus looked around and said to his disciples, "How hard it will be for those who have wealth to enter the kingdom of God!" And the disciples were perplexed at these words. But Jesus said to them again, "Children, how hard it is to enter the kingdom of God! It is easier for a camel to go through the eye of a needle than for someone who is rich to enter the kingdom of God." They were greatly astounded and said to one another, "Then who can be saved?" Jesus looked at them and said, "For mortals it is impossible, but not for God; for God all things are possible."*

Peter began to say to him, "Look, we have left everything and followed you." Jesus said, "Truly I tell you, there is no one who has left house or brothers or sisters or mother or father or children or fields, for my sake and for the sake of the good news, who will not receive a hundredfold now in this age—houses, brothers and sisters, mothers and children, and fields with persecutions— and in the age to come eternal life. But many who are first will be last, and the last will be first."

To contemplate:

The disciples are perplexed at Jesus' denial
  that wealth is God's great blessing;
they remember that Moses had said
  God blesses obedience to his commands
  with the riches of this world (Deut 28:1-6).

Wrong to want the good things God made?
  Then who in his wide world can be saved?
Why did God make this world and its wealth,
  if he wants us to give it all away?
Mark's Jesus is ever harder to grasp,
  first about Moses on divorce;
and now he proposes another dimension
  concerning the good of affluence,
    as a blessing of God himself.

Who can be saved if the lawful can't?
  Jesus admits that no one can:
"Impossible for humans but not for God.
  All things are within the power of God—
  You cannot save yourselves; *God can!*"

O Jesus, do you mean God made for us
  not only the world in which we live,
    but a much, much better world?
Do you mean we must give up our world
  to let God give us his better world—
    and let the last be first?

Along the Road to Death

Mark 10:32-34: *They were on the road, going up to Jerusalem, and Jesus was walking ahead of them; they were amazed, and those who followed were afraid. He took the twelve aside again and began to tell them what was to happen to him, saying, "See, we are going up to Jerusalem, and the Son of Man will be handed over to the chief priests and the scribes, and they will condemn him to death; then they will hand him over to the Gentiles; they will mock him, and spit upon him, and flog him, and kill him; and after three days he will rise again."*

To contemplate:

Once more he takes the uphill road
    toward the high point of his life—
Jerusalem, place where prophets die,
    city rising toward the sun.
Disciples suffer fear and dread,
    but Jesus walks straight on ahead.
Surely he knows the danger there,
    the trap the leaders set for him.

For he foretells: "The Son of Man
 will be condemned and handed up
to be mocked, scourged and spit upon—
 to death itself, dark death!"

Does he really see in such detail
 indignities that he will bear,
or is Mark now retrojecting them
 from knowing all that's come to pass?
Yet Jesus must know his present course
 will somehow bring him to his death,
but he presses on toward Jerusalem,
 to fulfill his Father's plan for him;
though the details may be dark indeed,
 he will not swerve a single step.
Jesus, how could you walk so bravely,
 so calmly, up to Jerusalem?

As I look upon my steepening road
 toward my own near-drawing death,
I marvel at your courage to climb
 along your uphill road.

One drop, Lord, give me a single drop
 of your steadfast valor,
to bear me along my own steep way
 into black night—with you....

Not to Be Served but to Serve

Mark 10:35-45: *James and John, the sons of Zebedee, came forward to him.... "Grant us to sit, one at your right hand and one at your left, in your glory." But Jesus said to them, "You do not know what you are asking. Are you able to drink the cup that I drink, or be baptized with the baptism that I am baptized with?" They replied, "We are able." Then Jesus said to them, "The cup that I drink you will drink; and with the baptism with which I am baptized, you will be baptized; but to sit at my right hand or at my left is not mine to grant, but it is for those for whom it has been prepared."*

When the ten heard this, they began to be angry with James and John. So Jesus called them and said to them, "You know that among the Gentiles those whom they recognize as their rulers lord it over them, and their great ones are tyrants over them. But it is not so among you; but whoever wishes to become great among you must be your servant, and whoever wishes to be first among you must be slave of all. For the Son of Man came not to be served but to serve, and to give his life a ransom for many."

To contemplate:

There they go again, the sons of thunder,
 shaking up a storm!
As soon as their Lord foretells his death,
 they make their brash request.
If he should die, then who will lead?
 Those to his right and left.

Can they pay the price to take his place:
 drink the cup that he will drink,
suffer the baptism he'll endure?
 They proudly claim they can.
Yes, they will finally give up their lives—
 That much he'll promise them!

But only the Father, who makes the plan,
 determines the place of honor.
As Jesus marches forward toward his end,
 he leaves all in his Father's hand.
The storm raised by the sons of thunder
 spreads to all the rest.
When two begin the climb toward fame,
 ambition stings the best.

O Jesus, you demand that we
 reverse the world's ideal:
instead of wanting to be served,
 we must want to serve.
 Only thus may we serve you!

"Jesus, Son of David!"

Mark 10:46-52: *As he and his disciples and a large crowd were leaving Jericho, Bartimaeus son of Timaeus, a blind beggar, was sitting by the roadside. When he heard that it was Jesus of Nazareth, he began to shout out and say, "Jesus, Son of David, have mercy on me!" Many sternly ordered him to be quiet, but he cried out even more loudly, "Son of David, have mercy on me!" Jesus stood still and said, "Call him here." And they called the blind man, saying to him, "Take heart; get up, he is calling you." So throwing off his cloak, he sprang up and came to Jesus. Then Jesus said to him, "What do you want me to do for you?" The blind man said to him, "My teacher, let me see again." Jesus said to him, "Go; your faith has made you well." Immediately he regained his sight and followed him on the way.*

To contemplate:

It's out at last,
    that noble title:
        "Son of David!"

No one till now
   has called him
      "Son of David."
Only the blind man in the street
   can see who Jesus is:
      David's long-awaited heir!

At Jesus' call the man
   throws off his cloak,
      leaps up and comes to him.
Such spirited response
   wins Jesus' own response:
      "Your faith has made you well."
And, sight restored,
   he follows David's son
      up toward Jerusalem.

Now that the word is out,
   the word he's David's son,
      he'll enter David's town,
ready now to culminate
   his whole life's work—
      his Father's mission.

Son of David, let me,
   like the blind man—
      let me follow you

         up to Jerusalem....

David's Son Enters His City

Mark 11:1-11: *When they were approaching Jerusalem...near the Mount of Olives, he sent two of his disciples and said to them, "Go into the village ahead of you, and immediately as you enter it, you will find tied there a colt that has never been ridden; untie it and bring it. If anyone says to you, 'Why are you doing this?' just say this, 'The Lord needs it and will send it back here immediately.'" They went away and found a colt tied near a door, outside in the street.... Then they brought the colt to Jesus and threw their cloaks on it; and he sat on it. Many people spread their cloaks on the road, and others spread leafy branches that they had cut in the fields. Then those who went ahead and those who followed were shouting,*

"Hosanna!

Blessed is the one who comes in the name of the Lord!

Blessed is the coming kingdom of our ancestor David!

Hosanna in the highest heaven!"

Then he entered Jerusalem and went into the temple.

To contemplate:

Jesus, who cured the blind man
 heralding him as "Son of David,"
now enters his ancestral city
 on the colt of a beast of burden.
No noble steed or polished arms,
 no splendid saddle-throne.
Only the colt of a beast of burden
 and disciples' cloaks to sit on.
This man so poor he has no colt
 must borrow one to come as king,
must promise to send it back at once—
 sorry figure of a king!

Yet many spread their cloaks for him,
 and wave before him leafy boughs;
and loudly shout that he's the one
 who comes in the sacred name of "Lord."
They sing the blessings of David's psalm (118:26),
 acknowledging that this poor man
comes to them in God's great name
 to bring back David's throne.

Lord, in the city of your heritage
 you go straight to your Father's house,
where you offer him your very life
 in royal humility.
O Son of David, I welcome you
to the temple of my heart!

Jesus Curses a Barren Fig Tree

Mark 11:12-26: *On the following day, when they came from Bethany, he was hungry. Seeing in the distance a fig tree in leaf, he went to see whether perhaps he would find anything on it. When he came to it, he found nothing but leaves, for it was not the season for figs. He said to it, "May no one ever eat fruit from you again." And his disciples heard it.*

Then they came to Jerusalem. And he entered the temple and began to drive out those who were selling and those who were buying.... "Is it not written,

'My house shall be called a house of prayer for all the nations'?

But you have made it a den of robbers...."

In the morning as they passed by, they saw the fig tree withered away to its roots. Then Peter remembered and said to him, "Rabbi, look! The fig tree that you cursed has withered." Jesus answered them, "Have faith in God. Truly I tell you, if you say to this mountain, 'Be taken up and thrown into the sea,' and if you...believe that what you say will come to pass, it will be done for you. So I tell you, whatever you ask for in prayer, believe that you have received it, and it will be yours. Whenever you stand praying, forgive, if you have anything against anyone; so that your Father in heaven may also forgive you."

To contemplate:

Mark's Jesus curses a hapless tree
  that offers him no fig to eat.
    Doesn't he know figs are out of season?
Has he gone mad from too much stress?
  Or have the hosannas made him think
    that even trees must please his whim?

His anger floods God's great temple;
  he drives out indiscriminately
    buyers and sellers.
Yet, is he moved by anger or grief
  for those who would steal
    forgiveness for unrepented sins,
    even as Jeremiah said (7:8-11)?

And there's the fig tree, withered now,
  withered, as Jeremiah warned—
    "When I wanted to gather them,
    says the Lord, there are...no figs
    on the fig tree" (8:13).

O Jesus, I, too, bear little fruit;
  I, too, am weighed down with heavy sins,
    like mountains I must cast away.
  I beg your Father's kind forgiveness,
    as I forgive my enemies.

Jesus' Authority

Mark 11:27-33: *Again they came to Jerusalem. As he was walking in the temple, the chief priests, the scribes, and the elders came to him and said, "By what authority are you doing these things? Who gave you this authority to do them?" Jesus said to them, "I will ask you one question; answer me, and I will tell you by what authority I do these things. Did the baptism of John come from heaven, or was it of human origin? Answer me." They argued with one another, "If we say, 'From heaven,' he will say, 'Why then did you not believe him?' But shall we say, 'Of human origin'?"—they were afraid of the crowd, for all regarded John as truly a prophet. So they answered Jesus, "We do not know." And Jesus said to them, "Neither will I tell you by what authority I am doing these things."*

To contemplate:

They demand of you, the Lord,
    an explanation.
They demand to know
    by what authority you act.

Are we not always thus
   with you, our Lord,
demanding you explain to us
   your every word and deed?

You offer to answer their demand,
   on one condition—
that they answer first a question
   about John the Baptist:
"By what authority did John proceed
   to baptize people?"
These leaders did not submit
   to John's demand.
Now they can ill afford to lose
   the trusting crowd
who do believe that John was sent
   to them by God.
So they resort to subterfuge:
   "We do not know."
Ah, Lord, you have them there!
   If they don't know that,
then how can they expect to know
   the more important fact—
the divine source of your
   absolute authority?

Jesus, my Lord, to you I bow,
embrace your loving sovereignty.

The Parable of the Tenants

Mark 12:1-12: *Then he began to speak to them in parables. "A man planted a vineyard, put a fence around it, dug a pit for the wine press, and built a watchtower; then he leased it to tenants and went to another country. When the season came, he sent a slave to the tenants to collect from them his share of the produce of the vineyard. But they seized him, and beat him, and sent him away empty-handed. And again he sent another slave to them; this one they beat over the head and insulted. Then he sent another, and that one they killed.... He had still one other, a beloved son. Finally he sent him to them, saying, 'They will respect my son.' But those tenants said to one another, 'This is the heir; come, let us kill him, and the inheritance will be ours.' So they seized him, killed him, and threw him out of the vineyard. What then will the owner of the vineyard do? He will come and destroy the tenants and give the vineyard to others. Have you not read this scripture:*

   'The stone that the builders rejected
     has become the cornerstone;
   this was the Lord's doing,
     and it is amazing in our eyes'?"

When they realized that he had told this parable

against them, they wanted to arrest him, but they feared the crowd. So they left him and went away.

To contemplate:

Isaiah portrayed God's people as a vineyard
  in which God worked to grow the best of grapes.
Instead, it yielded "wild grapes" (Is 5:2).
Mark's Jesus interprets the prophet's words
  and admonishes those
whom God had chosen to cultivate his vineyard.

And what of me?
How have I received the prophets
  God has sent into my life?
How have I received the Father's Son
  and brought his word to harvest in my heart?
Isaiah asked, "What more was there to do
  for my vineyard that I had not done?" (Is 5:4).

O Jesus, what more could you have done for us
  than give your life?
You braved your death despite the pain;
you went on, for love of us,
Straight on toward death on Golgotha!

The Emperor's Coin

Mark 12:13-17: *Then they sent to him some Pharisees and some Herodians to trap him in what he said. And they came and said to him, "Teacher, we know that you are sincere, and show deference to no one; for you do not regard people with partiality, but teach the way of God in accordance with truth. Is it lawful to pay taxes to the emperor, or not? Should we pay them, or should we not?" But knowing their hypocrisy, he said to them, "Why are you putting me to the test? Bring me a denarius and let me see it." And they brought one. Then he said to them, "Whose head is this, and whose title?" They answered, "The emperor's." Jesus said to them, "Give to the emperor the things that are the emperor's, and to God the things that are God's." And they were utterly amazed at him.*

To contemplate:

They keep trying to trap you, Lord,
    trying to catch you in your speech,
        discredit you before your people,
            turn them against you.

If you answer "No, don't pay the tax,"
   the people will love you for it;
      but the emperor's governor
         will hunt you down.
And if you answer "Yes, pay the tax,"
   the governor will like you very much;
      but the people will despise you,
         leave you in disgust.

No way to win?
   But winning is not your game.
      Truth is what you stand for,
         your only aim.
And the truth is—
   the emperor has brought peace;
      security must have its price,
         "So pay the tax."
But there's a deeper truth:
   God brings to us the greater peace,
      the inner peace of heart—
         "Adore your God."

O Jesus, greatest teacher of them all!
   Teach me your way to greatest peace.
      Teach me to seek my peace with those
         authorized to keep the peace.
      But teach me first to seek the peace
   only you and the Father can give to us.

A Question about the Resurrection

Mark 12:18-27: *Some Sadducees, who say there is no resurrection, came to him and asked him a question, saying, "Teacher, Moses wrote for us that 'if a man's brother dies, leaving a wife but no child, the man shall marry the widow and raise up children for his brother.' There were seven brothers; the first married and, when he died, left no children; and the second married her and died, leaving no children; and the third likewise; none of the seven left children. Last of all the woman herself died. In the resurrection whose wife will she be? For the seven had married her."*

Jesus said to them, "Is not this the reason you are wrong, that you know neither the scriptures nor the power of God? For when they rise from the dead, they neither marry nor are given in marriage, but are like angels in heaven. And as for the dead being raised, have you not read in the book of Moses, in the story about the bush, how God said to him, 'I am the God of Abraham, the God of Isaac, and the God of Jacob'? He is God not of the dead, but of the living; you are quite wrong."

To contemplate:

A curious case some Sadducees present
   as "proof" against the raising of the dead.
But Jesus says they simply have no case,
   for there's no need of marriage after death.
The dead, raised up by God to his new life,
   will have no need of either sons or daughters
in whom to live vicariously after death,
   for they themselves will live eternally.
Nor will they need the special love of spouse;
   they'll have the love of all the saints in God.

These Sadducees think they master all of scripture,
   yet Jesus says they understand it not.
For they believe not God's creative power,
   even to raise the dead to greater life.
If there's no resurrection of the dead,
   why did God identify himself to Moses
as the God of Abraham, Isaac, Jacob—
   God not of the dead but of these living?

O Father of Jesus, Father mine,
   God of living men and women,
I believe your Son's disclosure:
   you will raise us up with him!

Jesus, our resurrection and our life (Jn 11:25),
   if today I live and die in you,
   tomorrow I will also rise with you!

Two Great Commandments

Mark 12:28-34: *One of the scribes came near and... seeing that he [Jesus] answered them well, he asked him, "Which commandment is the first of all?" Jesus answered, "The first is, 'Hear, O Israel: the Lord our God, the Lord is one; you shall love the Lord your God with all your heart, and with all your soul, and with all your mind, and with all your strength.' The second is this, 'You shall love your neighbor as yourself.' There is no other commandment greater than these." Then the scribe said to him, "You are right, Teacher; you have truly said that 'he is one, and besides him there is no other'; and 'to love him with all the heart, and with all the understanding, and with all the strength,' and 'to love one's neighbor as oneself,'—this is much more important than all whole burnt offerings and sacrifices." When Jesus saw that he answered wisely, he said to him, "You are not far from the kingdom of God."*

To contemplate:

Of all the commandments
   counted in the Torah—
     which command is first among them all?

Who can say which one is greatest?
If any can, the one who answers all that
    his critics have thrown at him—
    this Jesus standing here—may answer
the most important question of them all.
This time Mark's Jesus answers straightaway;
    no fencing, no counter question first.
    The question has been fair and frank—
        so will the answer be.

"Love, only love is God's true will:
    love God himself wholeheartedly;
    then love all others as yourself—
love is all that you must do."
The scribe agrees and even adds
    that love's worth more than sacrifice.
    And for this answer Jesus says:
"Not far from the kingdom of God are you—
    for where love rules, God reigns."

O Jesus, open up my heart and soul,
    my mind and strength—open *me*
    to return the love God gave to me,
        still gives me every day.
And may this love flow out to all
    my brothers, sisters—every one.
    For in love's kingdom I would live
        with you, eternally!

David's Son

Mark 12:35-37: *While Jesus was teaching in the temple, he said, "How can the scribes say that the Messiah is the son of David? David himself, by the Holy Spirit, declared,*

'The Lord said to my Lord,
"Sit at my right hand,
until I put your enemies under your feet."'

David himself calls him Lord; so how can he be his son?" And the large crowd was listening to him with delight.

To contemplate:

Jesus, you have silenced all of those
   who would have silenced you;
and now you leave them no recourse
   but to do away with you.
The blind man called you David's son;
   Jerusalem's crowd did, too.
Your questioners would have none of that—
   You—the Anointed One?

And that is just what you now show,
    by quoting the psalm that David wrote,
inspired, you say, by the Holy Spirit,
    inspired to tell God's truth.
In this psalm great David wrote:
    "The Lord God said to my Lord,
sit here beside my own right hand;
    I place your enemies underfoot" (cf. 110:1).
And so, you wisely reason thus:
    "If David calls Messiah 'Lord,'
how can he also be his son?
    Can a man's son be his Lord?"
With this enigma you have confounded
    your questioners anew,
using terms of the scribes themselves
    to call David's son his Lord.
David's son, yet David's Lord,
    I acknowledge your rightful place
at the right hand of almighty God,
    your enemies underfoot.

> Jesus, I honor you as David's son,
>   I adore you as his Lord,
> Ruler of God's own kingdom,
>   even at God's right hand!
> O, rule my life, my Lord!

The Widow's Offering

Mark 12:38-44: *As he taught, he said, "Beware of the scribes, who like to walk around in long robes, and to be greeted with respect in the marketplaces, and to have the best seats in the synagogues and places of honor at banquets! They devour widows' houses and for the sake of appearance say long prayers. They will receive the greater condemnation."*

He sat down opposite the treasury, and watched the crowd putting money into the treasury. Many rich people put in large sums. A poor widow came and put in two small copper coins, which are worth a penny. Then he called his disciples and said to them, "Truly I tell you, this poor widow has put in more than all those who are contributing to the treasury. For all of them have contributed out of their abundance; but she out of her poverty has put in everything she had, all she had to live on."

To contemplate:

Jesus, what a contrast you draw here
   between the great ones of this world
      and the little ones!
I picture you, dear Lord, sitting there,
   watching the rich contribute wealth,
      there in the treasury.
I wonder if Peter winked at John or James
   when a poor widow put in her coins:
      two copper pennies.

Did Matthew signal Andrew, Philip, Thomas,
   to watch the engaging scene with him,
      the two-penny scene?
I wonder if Judas laughed or sneered
   to see her place that trifling gift
      into the treasury?

But you, dear Lord, see more than they—
   you see into the poor widow's heart,
      where her love lives.
You tell your twelve to look again,
   for those two coins were all she had—
      she gave everything!

O Lord of all, both great and small—
   loving Lord of little ones,
      give us humility!

Stand Firm to the End!

Mark 13:1-8: *As he came out of the temple, one of his disciples said to him, "Look, Teacher, what large stones and what large buildings!" Then Jesus asked him, "Do you see these great buildings? Not one stone will be left here upon another; all will be thrown down."*

When he was sitting on the Mount of Olives opposite the temple, Peter, James, John, and Andrew asked him privately, "Tell us, when will this be, and what will be the sign that all these things are about to be accomplished?" Then Jesus began to say to them, "Beware that no one leads you astray. Many will come in my name and say, 'I am he!' and they will lead many astray. When you hear of wars and rumors of wars, do not be alarmed; this must take place, but the end is still to come. For nation will rise against nation, and kingdom against kingdom; there will be earthquakes in various places; there will be famines. This is but the beginning of the birthpangs."

To contemplate:

How fleeting, the glory of this world!
    Jesus' prophetic vision

reveals the end of this great temple—
   no stone upon a stone.
And like it, all our own "great" works
   will topple or gather dust
of ages that will not remember
   either our works or us.

Important, then, to live the way
   he told us we must do;
for it is only he who knows
   the road that leads to God.
Many we meet along life's path
   who point the way to joy:
"Eat this, drink that, try drugs or sex;
   or simply take your rest."
Other siren voices warn of the end that
   great wars and earthquakes
will bring upon our wobbly planet,
   to blot our poor lives out.

Jesus, I will not heed the voice
   that promises false peace,
nor fear great nature's rampages
   that threaten us with death.
Rather, I'll view these natural "signs"
   as "birthpangs" of a better world
your Father has prepared for us—
   eternal life with you!

Endure and Be Saved!

Mark 13:9-13: *"As for yourselves, beware; for they will hand you over to councils; and you will be beaten in synagogues; and you will stand before governors and kings because of me, as a testimony to them. And the good news must first be proclaimed to all nations. When they bring you to trial and hand you over, do not worry beforehand about what you are to say; but say whatever is given you at that time, for it is not you who speak, but the Holy Spirit. Brother will betray brother to death, and a father his child, and children will rise against parents and have them put to death; and you will be hated by all because of my name. But the one who endures to the end will be saved."*

To contemplate:

> The disciples who heard this warning word
> were indeed beaten
> by rulers and kings
> for you!
> And through the centuries since this word
> your followers endured the same
> for spreading abroad
> good news.

Hunted, hated, questioned, whipped,
 they relied upon your Spirit
  to reply to judges
   for them.
They trusted in your most solemn word,
 "Who endures to the end is saved;
  but first bear pain
   and death."

All of us who believe and follow you
 must be ready to face a world
  that laughs at you—
   and us.
Even in the heart of our families
 we may be violently opposed
  and ridiculed—
   for you.

Dark mystery of sorrow and bleak death
 for following you, our Lord,
  who suffered first
   for us!

Spirit, enflame our love!

Our Fragmenting World

Mark 13:14-27: *"But when you see the desolating sacrilege...flee to the mountains; the one on the housetop must not go down or enter the house to take anything away; the one in the field must not turn back to get a coat.... For in those days there will be suffering, such as has not been from the beginning of the creation.... And if anyone says to you at that time, 'Look! Here is the Messiah!' or 'Look! There he is!'—do not believe it. False messiahs and false prophets will appear and produce signs and omens, to lead astray, if possible, the elect. But be alert; I have already told you everything.*

"But in those days, after that suffering,
the sun will be darkened,
  and the moon will not give its light,
and the stars will be falling from heaven,
  and the powers in the heavens will be shaken.

Then they will see 'the Son of Man coming in clouds' with great power and glory. Then he will send out the angels, and gather his elect from the four winds, from the ends of the earth to the ends of heaven."

To contemplate:

Images portending doom—
  prophecies of dire destruction!
Desolating sacrilege,
  a world engulfed in sin.
A picture of our world today,
  a world which seems to say
that good is bad and bad is good,
  wrong is right and right, wrong.

Is our world of scientific progress
  a world falling apart—
sun and moon and earth darkened,
  stars falling out of the sky?
Are even our foundations shaken,
  common sense uncommon,
love hated, twisted, debased,
  till darkness seems our light?

O Lord, we are confused, dismayed,
  not ready for your coming.
Stay your angels yet, dear Lord,
  lest we be caught asleep!
We lie under your lovely stars,
  waiting for the sky to fall.
O Jesus, save us from the fate
  we bring upon ourselves!

"My Words Will Not Pass Away!"

Mark 13:28-37: *"From the fig tree learn its lesson: as soon as its branch becomes tender and puts forth its leaves, you know that summer is near. So also, when you see these things taking place, you know that he is near, at the very gates. Truly I tell you, this generation will not pass away until all these things have taken place. Heaven and earth will pass away, but my words will not pass away.*

"But about that day or hour no one knows, neither the angels in heaven, nor the Son, but only the Father. Beware, keep alert; for you do not know when the time will come. It is like a man going on a journey, when he leaves home and puts his slaves in charge, each with his work, and commands the doorkeeper to be on the watch. Therefore, keep awake—for you do not know when the master of the house will come, in the evening, or at midnight, or at cockcrow, or at dawn, or else he may find you asleep when he comes suddenly. And what I say to you I say to all: Keep awake."

To contemplate:

You said your words won't pass away—
 Yet you did not know the hour
your heavenly Father has decreed
 for the end of all the world.

I do believe your words are firm,
 steadfast as divinity;
yet, truly man, you knew not the hour—
 inscrutable mystery!

You have, indeed, gone on your journey,
 ascended to your Father's throne;
and now you know when you will come
 at the end of all the world.

I am awaiting your return,
 when I must give account
of all that I have said and done
 in the mission you've given me.

I know not when you'll come for me,
 at morn or noon or night.
But I need not fear if you're my judge—
 you're human, just like me.

Yet you have shown me how to live,
 fulfill my capabilities.
You warn us to keep wide awake—
 I dare not sleep, my Lord!

Jesus Is Anointed for Burial

Mark 14:1-9: *It was two days before the Passover and the festival of Unleavened Bread. The chief priests and the scribes were looking for a way to arrest Jesus by stealth and kill him....*

While he was at Bethany in the house of Simon the leper, as he sat at the table, a woman came with an alabaster jar of very costly ointment of nard, and she broke open the jar and poured the ointment on his head. But some were there who said to one another in anger, "Why was the ointment wasted in this way? For this ointment could have been sold for more than three hundred denarii, and the money given to the poor." And they scolded her. But Jesus said, "Let her alone; why do you trouble her? She has performed a good service for me. For you always have the poor with you, and you can show kindness to them whenever you wish; but you will not always have me. She has done what she could; she has anointed my body beforehand for its burial. Truly I tell you, wherever the good news is proclaimed in the whole world, what she has done will be told in remembrance of her."

To contemplate:

O Jesus, a shadow falls across your way—
    chief priests and scribes plot your death.
And now a second shadow darkens over you—
    a woman pours rich ointment on your head,
anointing you "for burial," portent of your death,
    the death you feel already on your path.

Worse yet, your own disciples think it waste—
    a waste to lavish care upon your body!
"Better," they say, "to sell the perfumed oil
    and give the proceeds to the poor."
They fail to see that serving you is serving them,
    that you yourself are poorer than the poor.
They have not seen death's shadow closing in;
    they fail to comprehend what's happening.
Undiscerning, they still do not understand
    that you are God's Anointed One—the Christ,
or realize how fittingly the woman reenacts
    Samuel's consecrating David king (1 Sam 16:13).
Yet she anoints you not for throne but tomb,
    not for life of fame but death of shame.
Three years you've worked among your people;
    three days, and they will nail you to a cross!

Jesus, I bow before your messianic face,
    dripping with the oil of your anointing!

The Passion and Resurrection

Passover Preparations

Mark 14:10-16: *Then Judas Iscariot, who was one of the twelve, went to the chief priests in order to betray him to them. When they heard it, they were greatly pleased, and promised to give him money. So he began to look for an opportunity to betray him.*

On the first day of Unleavened Bread, when the Passover lamb is sacrificed, his disciples said to him, "Where do you want us to go and make the preparations for you to eat the Passover?" So he sent two of his disciples, saying to them, "Go into the city, and a man carrying a jar of water will meet you; follow him, and wherever he enters, say to the owner of the house, 'The Teacher asks, Where is my guest room where I may eat the Passover with my disciples?' He will show you a large room upstairs, furnished and ready. Make preparations for us there." So the disciples set out and went to the city, and found everything as he had told them; and they prepared the Passover meal.

To contemplate:

Judas finally takes the leap
   into the blackness of betrayal—
      arrangements for your death.
The whole world now moves forward
   in maddening, headlong course
      toward momentous tragedy.

After such an act of betrayal
   could Passover preparations
      have meaning anew?
On the first day of Unleavened Bread
   Passover lambs are sacrificed—
      a symbol to us of you, the true Lamb.

You now send two of your disciples
   to prepare your final meal,
      your Passover meal to death!
This meal, recalling delivery
   of Israel from Egypt's slavery,
      will be your own Passover meal—
your supper promising delivery
   of your people from their sins,
      through Calvary's coming sacrifice.

Jesus, I kneel before your cross,
   marveling at your love for us....

Jesus Knows His Betrayer

Mark 14:17-21: *When it was evening, he came with the twelve. And when they had taken their places and were eating, Jesus said, "Truly I tell you, one of you will betray me, one who is eating with me." They began to be distressed and to say to him one after another, "Surely, not I?" He said to them, "It is one of the twelve, one who is dipping bread into the bowl with me. For the Son of Man goes as it is written of him, but woe to that one by whom the Son of Man is betrayed! It would have been better for that one not to have been born."*

To contemplate:

"It is one of the twelve!"
    One of twelve you chose from all the world
        has rejected you, turned against you.

And you sit there peaceful,
    tranquilly eating with the men you chose,
        with the one who chose to betray you.

They are amazed, disbelieving
   that one of them could fall so low.
      How could one of them betray you—

even one who hypocritically
   dips bread into the bowl in which you dip,
      violating the covenant of fellowship?

Yet, before I condemn poor Judas,
   I look into my own inconstant heart,
      and wonder about myself—
         could I betray you?

O Jesus, you know the changeling
   I have been throughout my years of life—
      how often I have sinned,
         how grievously.

Yet you've always waited there,
   waited for me to change again for you—
      to turn away from sin,
         return to you.

I resolve to betray you nevermore—
   never betray one who has been my friend,
      nor even enemy, betray—
         for I belong to you!

This Is My Body

Mark 14:22-26: *While they were eating, he took a loaf of bread, and after blessing it he broke it, gave it to them, and said, "Take; this is my body." Then he took a cup, and after giving thanks he gave it to them, and all of them drank from it. He said to them, "This is my blood of the covenant, which is poured out for many. Truly I tell you, I will never again drink of the fruit of the vine until that day when I drink it new in the kingdom of God." When they had sung the hymn, they went out to the Mount of Olives.*

To contemplate:

In the simple scene of that last supper meal
   you take the bread and wine of every day,
change them into your body and your blood
   and thereby give your very self to men.
Your body, Lord, your blood you give to them!
   Who could ever believe in such a gift?
Can they believe, the men you give this gift—
   even after seeing all your miracles?

You offer them flesh that will be torn tomorrow,
   and blood that will trickle down the cross;
you offer them your very self before you die,
   yourself as food and drink for them—as feast!
You give to those who disapproved the gift of her
   who poured the oil upon your head,
anointing you for suffering, death and burial—
   do they now disapprove your gift to them?

What do they think and feel as they receive
   your body to eat, your precious blood to drink?
How can they thank you for this last gift to them
   this very night before you die for them?
You know that when the soldiers come for you,
   one of these will guide them to your garden,
And all the rest will flee, abandoning you;
   their leader will deny he ever knew you.
Yet you give yourself—your flesh to eat,
   your blood to drink—to most unworthy men!

How can we thank you for that same gift of love—
   your gift of self, your body and your blood?
Only the body-blood that rose up from the tomb—
   your eternal self in glory absolute—
     only your Eucharistic self
        can be our thanks!

Jesus Knows They Will Desert Him

Mark 14:27-31: *And Jesus said to them, "You will all become deserters; for it is written,*
   'I will strike the shepherd,
      and the sheep will be scattered.'
   But after I am raised up, I will go before you to Galilee." Peter said to him, "Even though all become deserters, I will not." Jesus said to him, "Truly I tell you, this day, this very night, before the cock crows twice, you will deny me three times." But he said vehemently, "Even though I must die with you, I will not deny you." And all of them said the same.

To contemplate:

How could you give these fragile men,
   who will desert you and deny you,
      your flesh to eat and blood to drink?

You've spent three years preparing them,
   three years teaching them—to desert you?
      Three times their leader will deny you!

You know all this and tell them plainly.
>   Yet you are kind to them, and gentle,
>   reminding them you are their shepherd,
>   forgiving them, even before they sin.

Peter, of course, must have his own last word,
>   protesting he will go to die with you,
>   never even think of denying you—
>   Peter, the most daring of them all!

And what of me, O Jesus, what of me?
>   If they will desert and Peter will deny you,
>   how will I stay, how will I affirm you?
>   It takes so little to shock or frighten me
>   from following you along the path you set—
>   oh, what can you expect of me, my Lord?

I am indeed a wandering, errant sheep,
>   ready at the slightest hint of risk
>   to leave you for the merest dross.
>   Stoop, my Lord, stoop to my lowly state,
>   take me up into your shepherd arms,
>   close to your sacred heart of hearts.

>   I wait upon your love....

Abba, Not My Will but Yours

Mark 14:32-42: *They went to a place called Gethsemane; and he said to his disciples, "Sit here while I pray." He took with him Peter and James and John, and began to be distressed and agitated. And said to them, "I am deeply grieved, even to death; remain here, and keep awake." And going a little farther, he threw himself on the ground and prayed that, if it were possible, the hour might pass from him. He said, "Abba, Father, for you all things are possible; remove this cup from me; yet, not what I want, but what you want." He came and found them sleeping; and he said to Peter, "Simon, are you asleep? Could you not keep awake one hour? Keep awake and pray that you may not come into the time of trial; the spirit indeed is willing, but the flesh is weak." And again he went away and prayed, saying the same words. And once more he came and found them sleeping, for their eyes were very heavy; and they did not know what to say to him. He came a third time and said to them, "Are you still sleeping and taking your rest? Enough! The hour has come; the Son of Man is betrayed into the hands of sinners. Get up, let us be going. See, my betrayer is at hand."*

To contemplate:

At least a few of them, three of them,
>you might expect to pray with you.
Especially when you are so deeply grieved—
>even unto death.
But not one of them can even stay awake,
>not one alert enough to pray.
What a likely crew to change the world
>when you are gone!

How human are you on this worst of nights,
>how vulnerable, how weak, dear Lord—
admitting to your grieving unto death,
>*begging* men for help;
imploring that your Father, your own dear Abba,
>remove your cup of agony,
"the cup of staggering" great Isaiah promised
>God would take away (51:22).

But you know it is the cup of bitter grief
>we sinners force upon your Abba.
You know that in the end your love must take it
>from his loving hand.
Your love for us, your towering love for him,
>accepts the cup we have prepared,
offers to drink it all—to bitter dregs
>of awful hate.

>Your love subdues our hate!

Betrayal and Desertion

Mark 14:43-52: *Immediately, while he was still speaking, Judas, one of the twelve, arrived; and with him there was a crowd with swords and clubs, from the chief priests, the scribes, and the elders. Now the betrayer had given them a sign, saying, "The one I will kiss is the man; arrest him and lead him away under guard." So when he came, he went up to him at once and said, "Rabbi!" and kissed him. Then they laid hands on him and arrested him. But one of those who stood near drew his sword and struck the slave of the high priest, cutting off his ear. Then Jesus said to them, "Have you come out with swords and clubs to arrest me as though I were a bandit? Day after day I was with you in the temple teaching, and you did not arrest me. But let the scriptures be fulfilled." All of them deserted him and fled.*

A certain young man was following him, wearing nothing but a linen cloth. They caught hold of him, but he left the linen cloth and ran off naked.

To contemplate:

A kiss as the betraying sign!
   A kiss, nature's sign of blessed love,
      becomes symbol to betray.
"Rabbi," the title of respect
   given to teachers, Judas gives to you
      to signal your arrest.

Rough men lay violent hands on you
   to take you captive, shackled firm,
      no more to walk the roads.
Brave Peter draws his trusty sword,
   with mighty swing cuts off an ear—
      strong guard of God's own Son!

They've come with swords and clubs
   to snare the gentlest of all men,
      subdue and capture you.
You offer no resistance—even as you told
   others not to resist arrest—
      as the scripture had foretold.

And all your valiant followers
   leave you and run away,
      even in nakedness.

O Jesus, what would I have done?
   I, too, have left you all alone;
   I, too, have oft deserted you
      and run away—
         naked.

He Was Silent

Mark 14:53-61: *They took Jesus to the high priest; and all the chief priests, the elders, and the scribes were assembled.... Now the chief priests and the whole council were looking for testimony against Jesus to put him to death; but they found none. For many gave false testimony against him, and their testimony did not agree. Some stood up and gave false testimony against him, saying, "We heard him say, 'I will destroy this temple that is made with hands, and in three days I will build another, not made with hands.'" But even on this point their testimony did not agree. Then the high priest stood up before them and asked Jesus, "Have you no answer? What is it that they testify against you?" But he was silent and did not answer.*

To contemplate:

There you stand before the court
   on trial for your words,
   on trial for your life!
They presume to try the Son of Man,
   to try the Son of David,
   to try *the Son of God!*

They find "witnesses" willing to testify
   falsely against your words
   and your transparent life:
"I will destroy this temple made with hands."
   False! You really said:
"Destroy this temple, and in three days
   I will raise it up—
   the temple of my body!" (Jn 2:19-21).

Yes, men will destroy your Father's temple,
   the temple of your body,
   the temple of your Spirit.
And in three days, you will raise it up,
   the temple of your body,
   the temple of your Spirit.

But now you do not even try to answer them—
   they won't listen to your word;
   they didn't listen to your life.

You stand there saying nothing, silent,
   though you are harshly treated—
      as Isaiah had foretold:
   "He opened not his mouth" (53:7).

Jesus, I watch you stand there, silent....

He Deserves to Die!

Mark 14:61-65: *Again the high priest asked him, "Are you the Messiah, the Son of the Blessed One?" Jesus said, "I am; and*

> *'you will see the Son of Man*
> *seated at the right hand of the Power,'*
> *and 'coming with the clouds of heaven.'"*

Then the high priest tore his clothes and said, "Why do we still need witnesses? You have heard his blasphemy! What is your decision?" All of them condemned him as deserving death. Some began to spit on him, to blindfold him, and to strike him, saying to him, "Prophesy!" The guards also took him over and beat him.

To contemplate:

My Jesus, you are silent,
   till the high priest
      asks the right question.
Then, indeed, you speak,
   quoting Daniel's prophecy
      about the Son of Man (Dan 7:13-14).

Now we know, dear Lord,
> why you have been referring
>> to yourself as Son of Man!
You are that Son of Man
> who will come upon the clouds,
>> God's glorious clouds, as judge (Mt 25:31).
The high priest tears his clothes,
> despairing of your soul,
>> assuming you've blasphemed.
They all condemn you to your death—
> the Son of Man, our judge,
>> they judge "deserving death"!

And they begin to spit on you,
> vulgarly to spit on you—
>> spit on the Son of Man!
They play a blindfold game with you,
> the game of prophecy—
>> "Who struck you, *Lord?*"

O Jesus, be my own dear Lord:
> Lord of all my words,
>> Lord of all my life!
I kneel before you, Son of Man,
> and watch you let them
>> strike you....

Peter Denies His Lord

Mark 14:66-72: *While Peter was below in the courtyard, one of the servant-girls of the high priest came by. When she saw Peter warming himself, she stared at him and said, "You also were with Jesus, the man from Nazareth." But he denied it, saying, "I do not know or understand what you are talking about." And he went out into the forecourt. Then the cock crowed. And the servant-girl, on seeing him, began again to say to the bystanders, "This man is one of them." But again he denied it. Then after a little while the bystanders again said to Peter, "Certainly you are one of them; for you are a Galilean." But he began to curse, and he swore an oath, "I do not know this man you are talking about." At that moment the cock crowed for the second time. Then Peter remembered that Jesus had said to him, "Before the cock crows twice, you will deny me three times." And he broke down and wept.*

To contemplate:

Your chosen leader, Lord,
    the man you called the "Rock"—
        look at him now, Jesus.
    Is he still your "Rock"?

Even a servant-girl he fears,
　　fears her simple statement
　　　　that he was there with you.
　　Peter denies the truth.
He no longer wants to be with you,
　　nor be your disciple.
　　　　Just to be near you now
　　has become too great a risk.
No shock to you that the chief priests
　　and scribes desire your death;
　　　　no shock, the soldiers' game.
　　But that Peter denies knowing you!

Poor Peter, poor impetuous Peter
　　has forgotten your word to him.
　　　　But the second cock crow
　　shocks him back to reality.

He weeps, breaks down and weeps.
　　Yes, he is Peter after all,
　　　　the man who in the fishing boat
　　declared himself a sinner (Lk 5:8).

Jesus, I am much like Peter—
　　not Peter rock but Peter weak,
　　　　who failed to testify to you.
　　Dear Lord, I weep with him....

Jesus Before Pilate

Mark 15:1-5: *As soon as it was morning, the chief priests held a consultation with the elders and scribes and the whole council. They bound Jesus, led him away, and handed him over to Pilate. Pilate asked him, "Are you the King of the Jews?" He answered him, "You say so." Then the chief priests accused him of many things. Pilate asked him again, "Have you no answer? See how many charges they bring against you." But Jesus made no further reply, so that Pilate was amazed.*

To contemplate:

They bind you, Lord,
    bind you who have come
        to give them freedom.
They lead you away,
    lead you who would lead them
        to your Father's house.
But you they lead to Pilate
    to demand your slow death
        upon a Roman cross.

Pilate is no arbitrary fool;
   he asks, "Are you a king—
      are you the King of Jews?"
Your answer, O my king,
   in Hebrew affirmative,
      leaves Pilate wondering.
But at their accusations
   your silence amazes him.
      You're far beyond his grasp.

I picture you, my king,
   standing there in silence
      before the Roman governor,
nobler than your accusers,
   nobler than your judge—
      you stand there, king of both.
You stand again in silence,
   the silence of a king
      who has no need of words.

For all words fail before you;
   no word tells who you are,
      your true nobility.
   I kneel silently before you,
      my silent king!

Crucify Him!

Mark 15:6-14: *Now at the festival he [Pilate] used to release a prisoner for them, anyone for whom they asked. Now a man called Barabbas was in prison with the rebels who had committed murder during the insurrection. So the crowd came and began to ask Pilate to do for them according to his custom. Then he answered them, "Do you want me to release for you the King of the Jews?" For he realized that it was out of jealousy that the chief priests had handed him over. But the chief priests stirred up the crowd to have him release Barabbas for them instead. Pilate spoke to them again, "Then what do you wish me to do with the man you call the King of the Jews?" They shouted back, "Crucify him!" Pilate asked them, "Why, what evil has he done?" But they shouted all the more, "Crucify him!"*

To contemplate:

They cry for blood—
your blood, my Lord.
They cry for death—
your death, my king.

Pilate seeks a way
to save you from the cross.

He brings before the crowd
Barabbas and yourself.

Two stand before the mob,
a murderer and the Son of God—

one man would kill again,
and one would save them all.

And whom do they prefer,
murderer or Savior?

Are we so different now?
Whom do we select?

Barabbas the rebel
many of us still choose;

and Jesus the king
we still crucify.

And I? Whom do I choose,
murderer or Savior?

O Jesus, be my king,
my saving Lord and king!

No more would I rebel,
no more serve evil cause.

To pledge my loyalty,
I kneel before my king....

Jesus Is Scourged and Thorn-Crowned

Mark 15:15-20: *So Pilate, wishing to satisfy the crowd, released Barabbas for them; and after flogging Jesus, he handed him over to be crucified.*

Then the soldiers led him into the courtyard of the palace (that is, the governor's headquarters); and they called together the whole cohort. And they clothed him in a purple cloak; and after twisting some thorns into a crown, they put it on him. And they began saluting him, "Hail, King of the Jews!" They struck his head with a reed, spat upon him, and knelt down in homage to him.... They stripped him of the purple cloak and put his own clothes on him. Then they led him out to crucify him.

To contemplate:

O Jesus, they cruelly flog you,
   beat your back and shoulders
      with wicked Roman lash,
         tipped with jagged iron.

They tear into your back,
   make rivulets of blood
      run down your legs and feet,
         red pools upon the ground.
Rough soldiers cast upon you
   a purple cloak of scorn;
      cruel soldiers make a crown
         of twisted branch of thorn.
They bow and scrape before you,
   mocking your royal self,
      "Hail, glorious King of Jews,
         the one who'll save us all!"
They strike upon your head,
   drive deep the crowning thorns.
      They spit upon your face,
         and kneel "adoring" you.
When they have had their fun,
   they strip off cloak of clown,
      throw upon your bleeding back
         your own now tattered robe.

O Jesus, you have suffered so,
   borne all this agony,
      indignity and scorn—
         borne all this for me.
I look upon your bloodied face
   and wonder, wonder how
      I can return your love
         for sinful me....

The Crucifixion

Mark 15:21-26: *They compelled a passer-by, who was coming in from the country, to carry his cross; it was Simon of Cyrene, the father of Alexander and Rufus. Then they brought Jesus to the place called Golgotha (which means the place of a skull). And they offered him wine mixed with myrrh; but he did not take it. And they crucified him, and divided his clothes among them, casting lots to decide what each should take.*

It was nine o'clock in the morning when they crucified him. The inscription of the charge against him read, "The King of the Jews."

To contemplate:

They lead you out toward Golgotha,
   lead you through crowded streets
      of old Jerusalem.
Too weak to carry your own cross,
   you falter on your anguished way
      toward ugly Golgotha.
Anxious to see you mount the cross,
   they pass it to Simon of Cyrene,
      lest you die too soon!

Golgotha—that Place of Skull—
    appropriate for crucifixion
        and agonizing death!
Wine, drugged wine they offer you,
    a touch of unexpected mercy.
        But you refuse to drink.
You will not blot out suffering;
    you offer it to loving Father,
        to heal our brokenness.

They nail you to the cruel cross,
    fix you there against the sky,
        a curse for all to see (Gal 3:13).
Your executioners play games
    to win the clothes you wore—
        paid for with your life.
With a sign they tell the whole wide world
    just who you really are:
        "King of all the Jews."

O King of Jews and Gentiles both,
    my own king crucified,
        I bow in love for you—
        my crucified!

Come Down from Your Cross

Mark 15:27-32: *And with him they crucified two bandits, one on his right and one on his left. Those who passed by derided him, shaking their heads and saying, "Aha! You who would destroy the temple and build it in three days, save yourself, and come down from the cross!" In the same way the chief priests, along with the scribes, were also mocking him among themselves and saying, "He saved others; he cannot save himself. Let the Messiah, the King of Israel, come down from the cross now, so that we may see and believe." Those who were crucified with him also taunted him.*

To contemplate:

Three forlorn figures hang against the sky,
    heads drooping, arms outstretched
        in death-bound agony.
But all contempt is aimed at only one;
    they can't allow to die in peace
        the one who dies for them.

Those passing by revile him, jeer at him;
   they shake their heads and shout
      cruel words of irony:
"You who'd destroy the temple are destroyed.
   You who'd smash and rebuild all,
      come down and save yourself!"

The priests and scribes
   also shout, "Others he saved;
      he cannot save himself!
Let the Messiah king come down from the cross
   that we may see and then believe."

O Jesus, why hang there upon the cross
   for those who don't believe?
How powerfully you must now feel
   tempted to forsake the plan
      your Father has devised.

Yet there you hang until the end,
   hang there against the sky—
      for us who scarcely love.
Jesus, I watch you hang upon your cross,
   hang there for all of us,
      fixed in eternal love.

"My God, My God!"

Mark 15:33-34: *When it was noon, darkness came over the whole land until three in the afternoon. At three o'clock Jesus cried out with a loud voice, "Eloi, Eloi, lema sabachthani?" which means, "My God, my God, why have you forsaken me?"*

To contemplate:

The backdrop of the crucified grows dark;
   the wild world mourns in grief
at what is taking place on Golgotha—
   a world mourns the death of him
who was the pattern for its making.
   This lost world tries to hide from view
the torment of its brightest star.
   Or is it shame that hides its face
at desolate cry of the crucified:
   "Why have you forsaken me?"
Can the man who shouts out such a cry
   really be Lord of all the world?

How can God abandon God himself?
　　How can this dying man be God?
One thing is clear beyond all doubt—
　　Jesus is truly one of us:
he suffers all that we can suffer:
　　absence of the Ground we stand on—
no, not absence but mysterious silence,
　　the silence of our God within,
Ground of our being who keeps us all
　　from sinking into nothingness.

O Jesus, as you sink into the void—
　　the blank of being we call death—
do you feel the terror that we feel
　　at imminent nothingness?
Even this have you endured for us!
　　Of you Paul wrote, "Though being God,
he emptied self, obedient unto death,
　　even death upon a cross!" (Phil 2:6-8).

O Jesus, when I cannot see the light
　　to find the God who keeps me live;
Oh, then, Lord Jesus, let me cling
　　to you upon that ancient cross,
And cry with you to our dear Abba:
　　"My God, my God, forsake me not!"

Why Have You Forsaken Me?

Mark 15:34: *At three o'clock Jesus cried out with a loud voice, "Eloi, Eloi, lema sabachthani?" which means, "My God, my God, why have you forsaken me?"*

To contemplate:

What kind of God is this?
   What kind of Father-God
      abandons his own Son,
         hanging there upon a cross?
Is there a father living now
   who would forsake his only son
      in such a moment of great need,
         the moment of his dying breath?
Is this the God that Jesus said
   made his own sabbath day for us—
      the God who told his baptized one
         "You are my own beloved Son"?
Did this God transfigure you
   and send you Moses and Elijah—
      the God who called out from his cloud,
         "This is my own beloved Son"?

How can he now abandon you
   and leave you on the cross to die
      before this taunting, jeering crowd,
         like a criminal—to die?
Can you still call him "Abba dear"?
   Can you command our love for him
      with all our heart and soul and mind?
         How can we love this God?
Does he still shine within your face,
   covered with sweat and dripping blood?
      Is he tasting death along with you,
      even though he cannot die?
Oh, mystery of all mysteries—
   that God himself hangs on a cross
      to show us his great grief at sin,
         and his undying love for us!

O Jesus, support my faith with yours,
   expand my love with your great love
      to look to God in my own grief
         and cry to him for our dying world—
      a world he never will forsake;
         for it contains his Son!

Jesus Died

Mark 15:34-38: *Jesus cried out with a loud voice, "Eloi, Eloi, lema sabachthani?" which means, "My God, my God, why have you forsaken me?" When some of the bystanders heard it, they said, "Listen, he is calling for Elijah." And someone ran, filled a sponge with sour wine, put it on a stick, and gave it to him to drink, saying, "Wait, let us see whether Elijah will come to take him down." Then Jesus gave a loud cry and breathed his last. And the curtain of the temple was torn in two, from top to bottom.*

To contemplate:

In your cry upon the cross, dear Lord,
   I hear the cry of all our race
accusing God of forsaking us,
     the men and women down the years
        who have forsaken God.
We, O God, have abandoned you.
   The cry upon the cross should be,
"My God, why have *we forsaken you?*"
     For Jesus cries in place of all
       for whom he enters death.

My God, I have forsaken you!
   I look upon my dying Lord,
and ask forgiveness through his voice
   crying out in darkness black
     for your forgiving love.
I hear my Jesus' last loud cry
   with final breath of life—
a cry that penetrates dark clouds,
   and tears the sanctuary veil,
     that hid from us our God.

And yet the silence deepens,
   the silence of his death.
Now not only God is silent;
   now our brother Jesus, too,
     hangs silent on his cross.
O Father, you so love our world,
   you give your only Son—
give him up to death for us
   as proof of love beyond
     your love that gave us birth.
In silence I look at love,
   at Love upon his cross—
     hanging in silent death....

"This Man Was God's Son!"

Mark 15:39-41: *Now when the centurion, who stood facing him, saw that in this way he breathed his last, he said, "Truly this man was God's Son!"*

There were also women looking on from a distance; among them were Mary Magdalene, and Mary the mother of James the younger and of Joses, and Salome. These used to follow him and provided for him when he was in Galilee; and there were many other women who had come up with him to Jerusalem.

To contemplate:

Even the hard centurion
   discovers in Jesus' death
      the secret of his identity:
         "This man was God's own Son!"
The very manner of his death
   reveals to his executioner
      the source of his mystery:
         "This man was God's own Son!"

Something in his long last breath—
   something beyond all cognizance,
      like the very breath of God,
         creative of new life.
For though the body now hangs limp,
   something there was about the way
      this man has died upon his cross—
         as no mere man can die.
As no man else he'd asked his God,
   "Why have you forsaken me?"
      What man could speak to God like that;
         then die most tranquilly?

Faithful women who followed him
   through all of Galilee,
      caring for his every need,
         do not desert him now.
They watch his body hanging there,
   stunned to see it without life,
      the body that gave so much life
         to so many sick and dying.

I join these women watching there,
   lost in silent wonder,
      thinking nothing,
         feeling nothing—
            just gazing silently....

Burial

Mark 15:42-47: *When evening had come, and since it was the day of Preparation, that is, the day before the sabbath, Joseph of Arimathea, a respected member of the council, who was also himself waiting expectantly for the kingdom of God, went boldly to Pilate and asked for the body of Jesus. Then Pilate wondered if he were already dead; and summoning the centurion, he asked him whether he had been dead for some time. When he learned from the centurion that he was dead, he granted the body to Joseph. Then Joseph bought a linen cloth, and taking down the body, wrapped it in the linen cloth, and laid it in a tomb that had been hewn out of the rock. He then rolled a stone against the door of the tomb. Mary Magdalene and Mary the mother of Joses saw where the body was laid.*

To contemplate:

Now that he is dead,
    they hasten to serve him.
Now that it makes no difference to him,
    Joseph reclaims his body!

Dead body...lifeless.
    Why bother now with details,
now that this world is over?
    What can you do when your world is dead?

They want to keep the sabbath law,
    and bury Jesus' body before the sun will set.
But what difference does it make
    to him hanging limp upon a tree?

Yet if we loved him while alive,
    we must revere his body—
at least provide it decent burial,
    in linen cloth and tomb.
They lay him in the tomb so dark,
    then roll the sealing stone.
Two Marys sit nearby and watch,
    watch where he's been put.

And with these Marys I will wait,
    keep watchful wake for him
        who died for me.
My Love is in the tomb....
    But the world's not over yet—
        it breathes expectantly!

He Has Been Raised!

Mark 16:1-6: *When the sabbath was over, Mary Magdalene, and Mary the mother of James, and Salome bought spices, so that they might go and anoint him. And very early on the first day of the week, when the sun had risen, they went to the tomb. They had been saying to one another, "Who will roll away the stone for us from the entrance to the tomb?" When they looked up, they saw that the stone, which was very large, had already been rolled back. As they entered the tomb, they saw a young man, dressed in a white robe, sitting on the right side; and they were alarmed. But he said to them, "Do not be alarmed; you are looking for Jesus of Nazareth, who was crucified. He has been raised; he is not here."*

To contemplate:

He has been truly raised?
   But he died upon a cross—
      was buried in this tomb.
         How can he now be raised?

As he hung there upon the cross,
   the passers-by had jeered,
      "So you can destroy the temple
         and rebuild it in three days!"

Yet as he died, the temple veil
   was torn from top to bottom.
      His body was that temple veil
         hiding divinity.
The very tearing of his body,
   resulting in his death,
      now lets us see beyond the veil
         that hid his secret self!

He has been raised!
   Nor death, nor tomb
      now holds the secret
         he kept so well so long.
Human enough to die as we,
   yet more than human, he.
      Out of the tomb, again alive,
         his body has been raised!

O Jesus, you have died for me,
   and live for me again.
      Raised by God from even death—
         you must be God himself.
   I worship you as my true God—
      yet love you as man like me!

They Were Afraid

Mark 16:5-8: *A young man, dressed in a white robe...said to them, "Do not be alarmed; you are looking for Jesus of Nazareth, who was crucified. He has been raised; he is not here. Look, there is the place they laid him. But go, tell his disciples and Peter that he is going ahead of you to Galilee; there you will see him, just as he told you." So they went out and fled from the tomb, for terror and amazement had seized them; and they said nothing to anyone, for they were afraid.*

To contemplate:

"He has been raised!
   He is not here....
      Tell them he will see them
         again in Galilee!"
Who ever heard such thing?
   What could this word mean?
      They flee the empty tomb,
         gripped in silent fear.

O Mark, why don't you tell us more?
   Why end on note so negative

> to tell us thing so positive—
>> resurrection of our Lord?
> Why, instead of happy ending
>> with images of glory—
>>> why do you leave us wondering
>>>> why the women speak no more?
> Do you end on enigmatic note
>> to hint that those who testify
>>> to Jesus' resurrection
>>>> must suffer dearly for it?
> You leave us gravely pondering
>> the cost that will be ours—
>>> the cost of faithful witnessing
>>>> to good news of Jesus Christ.
> You end your version of good news
>> with challenge running deep:
>>> "Will you give witness to his love
>>>> no matter what the price?"

My risen Lord, with Mark I hold
the image of the angel's pledge:
"Jesus has gone to Galilee—
the Galilee of God's own land—
there you'll see him, as he said!"

Probably during the second century an editor added to Mark a "Longer Ending" (16:9-20), perhaps to bring this Gospel into greater harmony with the others that were gathered together in the formation of the New Testament. This "Longer Ending" has traditionally been accepted as a canonical part of Mark, and so defined by the Council of Trent.

They Did Not Believe

Mark 16:9-14: *Now after he rose early on the first day of the week, he appeared first to Mary Magdalene, from whom he had cast out seven demons. She went out and told those who had been with him, while they were mourning and weeping. But when they heard that he was alive and had been seen by her, they would not believe it.*

After this he appeared in another form to two of them, as they were walking into the country. And they went back and told the rest, but they did not believe them.

Later he appeared to the eleven themselves as they were sitting at the table; and he upbraided them for their lack of faith and stubbornness, because they had not believed those who saw him after he had risen.

To contemplate:

The men who walked through life with you
    were a very special breed—
not the kind who would believe
    whatever they were told.
They had seen you free Magdalene
    from seven plaguing demons—
yet when she saw you alive again,
    they would not believe.
And when the two who walked with you
    told of meeting you,
your chosen ones again stood firm
    in stubborn disbelief.
So you yourself appeared to them
    at their supper table,
as on that night before your death,
    when you gave your body-blood.
And now you sit again with them,
    restored to life once more—
no, not that life you lived before;
    now you offer new life to them,
        eternal risen life!

Lord, when we falter in our faith,
    be with us at our table,
the table of your sacrament,
    to share your life with us—
        eternal risen life!

They Went Forth and He Worked with Them

Mark 16:15-20: *And he said to them, "Go into all the world and proclaim the good news to the whole creation. The one who believes and is baptized will be saved; but the one who does not believe will be condemned. And these signs will accompany those who believe: by using my name they will cast out demons; they will speak in new tongues; they will pick up snakes in their hands, and if they drink any deadly thing, it will not hurt them; they will lay their hands on the sick, and they will recover."*

So then the Lord Jesus, after he had spoken to them, was taken up into heaven and sat down at the right hand of God. And they went out and proclaimed the good news everywhere, while the Lord worked with them and confirmed the message by the signs that accompanied it.

To contemplate:

"Go, tell the good news everywhere!"
   You gave them firm command.
      "Whoever believes and is baptized
        will certainly be saved."

O Lord, I too have heard your news,
    your good news of salvation.
        I have believed and been baptized,
            I trust in you for life.
Cast out the demons of desire,
    my selfishness and sin.
        Sharpen my tongue to speak your word,
            strengthen my heart to love.
For in this world in which I live,
    lurks many a deadly thing;
        poisonous thoughts and lethal acts
            would snatch away your life from me.
Be my protection through my days;
    from evil set me free.
        And give me grace to do the same
            for those you send to me.

Ascended to your Father's throne,
    you sit at his right hand,
        joining him in endless joy,
            yet living still with us.
Now that we have heard your word
    to bear it to all others,
        work with us, confirm our word
            with signs of your great love.

    Jesus, work with us!

Dear Mark:

Thanks for your Spirit-filled Gospel
    of Jesus Christ, our Lord!
Something of his own bright light
    shines through your every word.
Something of his hidden glory,
    though muted in your report,
glows mysteriously through your book,
    even its somber parts.

You hint at his ecstatic joy
    after John baptizes him—
he feels the presence of peaceful Dove
    hears voice of loving Father!
And you suggest his deep delight
    forgiving crippling sins,
freeing demon-ridden souls,
    and healing ailing bodies.

You portray his celebration
    of Levi's change of heart,
and his gathering of a family
    who listen to his word.

Yes, Mark, you've suggested images
   of Jesus' jubilation.

But much more sharply you have stressed
   dark pictures of his grief:
his joining John's long line of sinners,
   temptations in the desert;
his empathy for all the sick,
   and for tormented hearts;

above all, his tragic loneliness
   as he keeps his inmost secret—
endures suspicions of his kin,
   indifference of his people,
misunderstanding of his disciples,
   censure of the priests.

Thanks for revealing his human love
   in his vulnerability!

O Jesus,
You shared our failures and our dreams,
   our anger at injustice, too,
our grief when betrayed and then denied—
   heartache from stony hearts.
You could not get the crowds to change,
   or all scribes and Pharisees to hear,
or even all your disciples to embrace
   the wisdom words you spoke.

And when it seemed that a few
   might penetrate your secret self,
they captured you, brought you to trial—
   and so you died upon a cross!

You were so human that you died;
   but not an ordinary death—
a death in lonely failure, yours,
   a death in total isolation,
   even from Abba, God himself.
Yet in that lonely death your peace
   convinced your executioner
he had killed the Son of God!
Then on the first day of the week
   the women found your empty tomb!

As on the first day of creation,
   God made light shine out of night,
made new life spring up from death—
   your glorious risen life, my Lord!

Jesus, with Mark, I believe in you.
   Like him I contemplate your life,
bear witness to your endless love
   that nailed you to the cross for us.
   With Mark, I hail your empty tomb.

With Mark, I firmly do resolve,
   no matter what the cost to me,
to place in you my final hope,
   and follow you untiringly.
Mark's Jesus and my own dear Lord,
   I love you everlastingly!

BOOKS & MEDIA

The Daughters of St. Paul operate book and media centers at the following addresses. Visit, call or write the one nearest you today, or find us on the World Wide Web, www.pauline.org

CALIFORNIA
3908 Sepulveda Blvd., Culver City, CA 90230; 310-397-8676
5945 Balboa Ave., San Diego, CA 92111; 619-565-9181
46 Geary Street, San Francisco, CA 94108; 415-781-5180

FLORIDA
145 S.W. 107th Ave., Miami, FL 33174; 305-559-6715

HAWAII
1143 Bishop Street, Honolulu, HI 96813; 808-521-2731

ILLINOIS
172 North Michigan Ave., Chicago, IL 60601; 312-346-4228

LOUISIANA
4403 Veterans Memorial Blvd., Metairie, LA 70006; 504-887-7631

MASSACHUSETTS
Rte. 1, 885 Providence Hwy., Dedham, MA 02026; 781-326-5385

MISSOURI
9804 Watson Rd., St. Louis, MO 63126; 314-965-3512

NEW JERSEY
561 U.S. Route 1, Wick Plaza, Edison, NJ 08817; 732-572-1200

NEW YORK
150 East 52nd Street, New York, NY 10022; 212-754-1110
78 Fort Place, Staten Island, NY 10301; 718-447-5071

OHIO
2105 Ontario Street (at Prospect Ave.), Cleveland, OH 44115; 440-621-9427

PENNSYLVANIA
9171-A Roosevelt Blvd., Philadelphia, PA 19114; 215-676-9494

SOUTH CAROLINA
243 King Street, Charleston, SC 29401; 843-577-0175

TENNESSEE
4811 Poplar Ave., Memphis, TN 38117 901-761-2987

TEXAS
114 Main Plaza, San Antonio, TX 78205; 210-224-8101

VIRGINIA
1025 King Street, Alexandria, VA 22314; 703-549-3806

CANADA
3022 Dufferin Street, Toronto, Ontario, Canada M6B 3T5; 416-781-9131
1155 Yonge Street, Toronto, Ontario, Canada M4T 1W2; 416-934-3440

¡Libros en español!